THE COMPLETE
Beyond the Fringe

The Complete
BEYOND THE FRINGE

Alan Bennett
Peter Cook
Jonathan Miller
Dudley Moore

With an Introduction
by **Michael Frayn**
Edited by **Roger Wilmut**

A Methuen Paperback

A METHUEN PAPERBACK

The main text of *Beyond the Fringe*
was first published in Great Britain
in 1963 by Souvenir Press Ltd
34 Bloomsbury Street, London WC2

This corrected and augmented edition
first published in 1987
by Methuen London Ltd
11 New Fetter Lane, London EC4P 4EE

Printed in Great Britain

British Library Cataloguing in Publication Data
The Complete beyond the fringe – (Methuen
    humour classics)
I. Bennett, Alan, *1934–*   II. Wilmut, Roger
828'.91409   PR6052.E5

ISBN 0–413–14670–7

Contents

Introduction

Beyond the Fringe first fell upon London like a sweet, refreshing rain on the tenth of May, 1961. It must have been St Jonathan's Day, because it rained satire thereafter, day and night, harder and harder, spreading outwards from London to cover the whole of the British Isles in one steady downpour of soaking jokes, until, as Peter Cook said, the entire realm seemed about to sink sniggering beneath the watery main.

It was the official opening of the Satirical Sixties. The demand must have existed, ravenous but unrecognised, before the supply was connected, because the public did not have to be coaxed to appreciate *Beyond the Fringe*. Conceivably, after ten years of stable Conservative government, with no prospect in 1961 of its ever ending, the middle classes felt some vague guilt accumulating for the discrepancy between their prosperous security and the continuing misery of those who persisted in failing to conform, by being black, or mad, or old. Conceivably they felt the need to disclaim with laughter any responsibility for this situation, and so relieve their consciences without actually voting for anything which might have reduced their privileges.

Why ever it was, audiences fell upon the show deliriously, like starving men, sweeping with them in the stampede all sorts of people who can scarcely have had much idea what it was they were devouring. I was in the audience on the second night, and everyone – myself included – was already inclined to hysteria. The couple in front of me, a perfectly sound pair of young Tories, were right with us, neighing away like demented horses, until the middle of Peter Cook's lampoon on Macmillan, when the man turned to the girl and said in an appalled whisper, 'I say! This is supposed to be the Prime Minister,' after which they sat in silence for the rest of the evening. God knows what cherished family prejudices they had betrayed by then.

God knows, for that matter, how the Lord Chamberlain ever came to allow the show to be put on. I have heard it suggested that there was a new spirit of enlightenment abroad in the Lord Chamberlain's office. I wonder. One of the few remarks his office made on the script when it was submitted to them, I gather, concerned the 'Bollard' number. Pointing out that it was the policy of the Lord Chamberlain not to allow the representation of homosexuality on the London stage, it suggested that the stage direction at the beginning of the number, which then read *'Enter two outrageous old queens'*, would be acceptable if it was amended to *'Enter two aesthetic young men'*. I suppose it saved the prompter from corruption.

In fact, by no means everything in *Beyond the Fringe* is satire, in the sense in which that poor broken-winded word has come to be understood. It has come to imply the slaughter of what are loosely called 'sacred cows', and the undermining of what is even more loosely called 'the Establishment'. But not all that much slaughter or undermining occurred in *Beyond the Fringe*. Several of the items – Jonathan Miller's monologue on the trousers, for instance – are clearly in the old whimsical-fantastical school of Paul Jennings and *Cranks* in which all Cambridge humorists of my generation were brought up. What seemed to me the best item of all – 'Bread Alone' – is an insane caricature of everyday social behaviour. The significant thing about them is that almost without exception they made one laugh until one's face ached.

I'm sure it was also largely the sheer surprise of going to a revue and finding oneself addressed not by hired spokesmen, zombies with neatly-organised theatrical faces, repeating someone else's jokes, but directly, by recognisable human beings, who talked about things that human beings talk about outside the theatre, and not special defunct demonstration topics brought out of the formaldehyde only for revues. It was also, after all the years of being nervously nursed back to sobriety after each joke with torch-songs and *pas de trois* representing jealousy, the grateful shock of finding that the management trusted one not to dislocate one's jaw or be sick over the furnishings if one was allowed to laugh continuously for the whole evening.

I say all this with hindsight. Indeed, it all seems absolutely obvious now. It was not obvious before it was done (even though Flanders and Swann had made some of the reforms already). Not to the producers of revues, at any rate. Nor, I may say, to me. I made some small and highly unsuccessful efforts to write revues once upon a time, and never once did it enter my head to try (for example) doing without the torch numbers. Revue had more or less strangled itself in its own clichés; the 'Fringe' people were the first in this country with the genuine originality to hack their way right back to first principles and start all over again. Alan Bennett once told me that they had conceived *Beyond the Fringe* simply by all standing round and deciding what they loathed, then sending it up. It sounds almost too admirably rational to be true.

After *Beyond the Fringe* the great flood of New Satire became more vitriolic. Most of it, however, sieved through the multiple strainers of mass communications, was broken down into a pale, watery substance with occasional mildly dirty jokes floating in it. In either case, the general direction it went from the 'Fringe' was steadily downhill. A good deal of it worked its way right back down to those marshes of stagnant cliché to which, on a May night in 1961, it seemed impossible that we should ever have to return.

What the show's imitators failed to observe was that such slaughter and demolition as it did contain were devastating firstly because they were done with wit, and secondly because they outraged the hitherto generally accepted convention that such things should not be done as public entertainment. The show made its audience laugh at the unthinking attitudes of respect which up till then they themselves had shared. Once it had annihilated the convention, to go *on* mocking the so-called Establishment has more and more meant making the audience laugh not at themselves at all, but at a standard target which is rapidly becoming as well-established as mothers-in-law. To do this is not to undermine but to confirm the audience's prejudices, and has less in common with satire than with community hymn-singing – agreeable and heart-warming as that may be.

It's also much less funny.

Michael Frayn

List of Illustrations

All the illustrations, with the exception of the frontispiece, are photographs by Zoë Dominic of the production which opened at the Fortune Theatre in May 1961.

Editor's Note to this edition

The main part of this book is devoted to presenting as accurately as possible the text of *Beyond the Fringe* as it was performed at the Fortune Theatre from May 1961 onwards. However, there were in fact five versions of the show, each having a slightly different selection of sketches, and a selection from the additional material is included, in Appendices 2 and 3.

The different versions of the show were as follows: a: The original hour-long version which opened as part of the Edinburgh Festival on 22 August 1960; b: A substantially revised and longer version which ran for a week at Cambridge, starting on 21 April 1960, and a week at Brighton, starting on 1 May 1961; c: the most famous version of the show opened at the Fortune Theatre, London, on 10 May 1961, being a shortened version of the Cambridge edition. It ran for over a year with the original cast, and then with a substitute cast until September 1966; d: The original cast opened in a version having minor revisions and additions at the John Golden Theatre, New York, on 27 October 1962; this is referred to as the 'Broadway version' in the Appendices. It ran for about a year; e: In September 1964 a new version, with substantial additions and alterations, opened on Broadway with Paxton Whitehead replacing Jonathan Miller. (However in the scripts of sketches from this version Miller's name has been used on the grounds that Whitehead was *acting* the part of Jonathan Miller.) This is referred to as the '1964 Broadway' version in this book.

The original London text was previously published by the Souvenir Press in 1962; however this version, which was based on the stage manager's copy, contains some errors and misprints, some of which recur in the edition of the Broadway version (which also included the 1964 additions) published by Samuel French.

In assembling the present text the previously published version has been checked against the text submitted to the Lord Chamberlain for censorship (and now held in the British Library as part of the Lord Chamberlain's Archive) and the gramophone records of some of the sketches. Where there are differences, the gramophone records are usually given precedence as representing what was actually said, even if only on that one occasion. In the case of the main text, the object has been to produce a version representing as accurately as is now possible the show as it was performed early in its London run. The Alan Bennett solo given here ('Let's Face It') is a different version from the previously published one; Bennett varied this sketch considerably during the run of the various versions of the show; this one comes from the Cambridge edition. That sketch and some of the sketches in the appendices, particularly those from the earlier versions, have come from the Lord Chamberlain's Archive without the possibility of further checks against recordings; but all the material has been checked over by the original cast.

(The material from the Lord Chamberlain's Archive is available to holders of the appropriate British Library Tickets; it is in the manuscript collection under the reference numbers LCP60/27 [Edinburgh] and LCP61/24 [Cambridge: the material was not re-submitted for the London version].)

Appendix 1 consists of an essay giving something of the history and background to the show; Appendix 2 contains the additional material written for the Broadway versions; Appendix 3 contains a small selection from the earlier versions of the show; details of the gramophone records are given in Appendix 4, the music for 'Man Bites God' and 'So That's the Way You Like It' is given in Appendix 5 and the book ends with postscripts by Alan Bennett, Dudley Moore and Peter Cook.

Roger Wilmut

13

Beyond the Fringe

1:   Steppes in the Right Direction

Jonathan, Peter and Alan are sitting or standing around the stage as the curtain rises. Dudley enters, walks to piano, sits down and plays the National Anthem. The other three all stand. Dudley goes off and the others sit down.

Peter   Who is that fellow who keeps coming in and playing 'God Save the Queen'?

Jon   I don't know, but he's obviously not English. No Englishman would keep coming in and playing it like that.

Alan   He's not English, certainly.

Jon   You can tell by the way he plays the whole thing sitting down.

Peter   Do you know what I think he is?

Jon   No, what do you think he is?

Peter   I think he is a member of the Moscow State Circus.

Jon   What makes you think that?

Peter   Well, I was in the washroom the other day and I was chatting to him – he was developing some photographs or something at the time – and I asked what he was doing over here, and he said: 'I am a member of the Moscow State Circus.' So I put two and two together. The whole thing added up to his being a member . . .

All   . . . of the Moscow State Circus.

Alan   He's an awfully nice fellow.

All   He's an absolute sweetie.

Alan   But I do wish he wouldn't keep coming in and playing 'God Save the Queen'.

Jon   I agree with you – I mean, I like the National Anthem. I like to start the day with the National Anthem.

Peter   Exactly – but every other minute of the day . . . I prefer a more sedentary way of life, myself.

Alan   It's probably because they get so very little chance to play it over there.

Jon   It's amazing how little their Bolshevism has contaminated their music.

Peter   Practically not at all – they play like absolute angels.

Jon & Alan   Absolute angels. Absolute Engels.

Peter   We could do with some of them over here.

All   Oh, we could indeed.

Peter   I tell you what, next time he comes in why don't we grab him and try and indoctrinate him – win him over to our point of view. Jonathan, you lie doggo over there. Alan, you lull his suspicions, look fat and contented – symbolise the British way of life. And I'll be behind this hat-stand here. *Cave*, chaps, here he comes. He could be a bit . . .

Dudley enters. He sees Peter, who pretends to be dusting the hat-stand. They all rush forward and grab Dudley.

Peter   Hello, there's a bit of dust on this hat-stand I was just . . . Right . . . Hello, there. Sit down, we're quite friendly – welcome to our lovely land, we hope you'll be very happy. No need to be alarmed.

Alan   You'll have to shout at him – they don't speak a word of English.

Peter   (*deliberately*) We in this country enjoy a high standard of living, with a considerable measure of political freedom . . .

Alan   Under the National Health Service for twelve shillings a week we are treated absolutely free.

Peter   Having any effect?

Jon   No, he's quite impervious. We'll have to try shock tactics.

Peter   Shock tactics – what do you suggest? (*To Dudley*) You stay here.

Alan, Peter and Jon whisper together.

Peter   Oh, yes. (*To Dudley*) Hello there, Russian Man. Now, you listen to me – I'm going to say something that will change your whole ideology. Just you listen to me. Khrushchev – (*raspberry*).

Jon   All right, all together. Khrushchev – (*raspberry*), Khrushchev – (*raspberry*). No, it's no good. It's not positive enough.

Alan   It's too negative.

Jon   Far too negative. Why not offer him something positive from our own culture – something encouraging from our own way of life to persuade him to join us.

Peter   What have we got? I know – a trump card! (*To Dudley*) Now you listen again, Russian Man. I want you to say after me these words – it's quite simple. Macmillan – (*smiling*) mmmmm. Now you have a shot. It's good fun. Macmillan – *mmmmm*.

Dudley   (*at the same time*) . . . (*raspberry*).

Peter   Macmillan – *mmmmm*.
Dudley (*at the same time*) . . . (*raspberry*).
Peter   Macmillan – *mmmmm*. Smile, you . . .
Alan   No, it's no use. Macmillan's obviously too bitter a pill to swallow first time.
Jon   All right. Let's start with something harmless or innocuous that he can't possibly take exception to . . . like Lord Snowdon . . . and work up slowly into a climax and hit him with it.
Peter   All right, you set the ball rolling, would you?
Jon   Yes. Right then. Something really fatuous to begin with. C. P. Snow – *mmmmm*.
Alan   Rule Britannia – *mmmmm*.
Peter   Arnold Wesker – *mmmmm*.
Jon   Henley Regatta – *mmmmm*.
Alan   Abide With Me – *mmmmm*.
Peter   This sea-girt isle – *mmmmm*.
Jon   Ian Fleming – *mmmmm*.
Alan   T. S. Eliot – *mmmmm*.
Peter   Robin Hood – *mmmmm*.
Jon   Never had it . . .
Alan   . . . so good . . .
All   Macmillan – *mmmmm*.
Dudley (*at the same time*) . . . (*raspberry*).
Peter   No, you don't seem to understand at all. It's Khrushchev – (*raspberry*). It's Macmillan – *mmmmm*.
Dudley (*at the same time*) . . . (*raspberry*).
Peter   No, Macmillan *mmmmm*.
Dudley (*at the same time*) . . . (*raspberry*).
Peter   Macmillan – (*raspberry*). Do you know, I think he's got something.
Jon   Macmillan – (*raspberry*) . . . Macmillan – (*raspberry*). Well, I must admit it's got a certain lilt to it.
Alan   Macmillan (*raspberry*). It's short but it's catchy.
All   (*singing to the tune of 'The Volga Boatmen'*)
             MACMILLAN – (*raspberry*).
             MACMILLAN – (*raspberry*).
             (*Dudley joins in on the piano*)
             MACMILLAN – (*raspberrry*).
             MACMILLAN *HOY!*

2: Royal Box

Two chairs are placed centre, facing upstage. Dudley sits on one.
Peter slips over his feet as though getting to a seat in a theatre, and
sits on the other chair.

Peter No, I won't have a programme, thank you very much. Excuse me, is this P – row P?

Dudley Yes, P 1, 2 and 3.

Peter I'm P 3.

Dudley I'm P 2.

Peter I'm most frightfully sorry, I got held up at the Haymarket, all the lights were against me.

Dudley That's all right. You've only missed three and a half minutes of the overture. It's a seven and a half minute overture, actually.

Peter I see, you've seen this show before, have you?

Dudley Oh, yes, I've seen this show, let me see now – 500, no, I tell a lie, 497 times.

Peter 497 times – that must be some sort of a record. Are you that fond of the show.

Dudley Oh no, it's not my sort of show at all, really.

Peter Well, why on earth do you keep coming?

Dudley Well you see, it's the Royal Family.

Peter The Royal Family – are they in some way connected . . .

Dudley No, no – you see, I read in the newspapers that the Royal Family was planning a visit to this theatre, so naturally I came along. You see, up there, that's what they call the Royal Box. But I don't know if you've noticed, there's no Royal People in it at the moment. No Royalty there at all. No Royal Personage actually gracing the Royal Box . . . unless of course they're crouching. But, I mean, that wouldn't be Royalty, would it?

Peter Not crouching, no.

Dudley No, not on the crouch.

Peter Not on the crouch, they don't go in for that very much.

Dudley But anyway, last Tuesday I was here and I saw, believe it or not, I saw the Duchess of Glastonbury.

Peter The Duchess of Glastonbury – well, lucky old you.

Dudley In fact, I mean she's not really what you'd call *regal*, is she?

Peter I suppose the Duchess of Glastonbury's more what you'd call *noble* rather than regal.

Dudley Yes, noble rather than regal, but you don't hold it against her, do you? No. Anyway, I am hoping against hope that one night the Royal Family will turn up and make my having to sit through this rotten awful show every night worth while.

Peter Do you really mean to say you spend twelve-and-sixpence every night just on the off-chance you may catch a glimpse of the Royal Family?

Dudley Well, they're not worth the fifteen shillings.

3: Man Bites God

Jon (*in darkness*) The time is 7 o'clock! By the Grace of God and Associated-Rediffusion, we bring you 'Always on a Sunday'! A programme of religion on the move. Let there be light!

The lights come up.

Dudley (*singing*) If your baby does you wrong*
Turn the other cheek
Keep it turning, turning, turning, turning
Love thy neighbour as thyself
Turn the other cheek.

Now if the Law starts getting stroppy
Don't think you are soppy
If you turn the other cheek
Oh keep it turning, turning, turning, turning . . .

Jon Thank you. Jolly good, boys. Thank you very much – that was really spiffing. It really had my feet tapping. Now, let's get down to God. God. Who is he, where is he, and above all, why is he – and of course, why is he above all? Now, Dudley, have you any questions you would like to fire off about God?

Dudley Yes . . . well, Vicar . . .

Jon Don't call me Vicar – call me Dick – that's the sort of Vicar I am!

Dudley gives him a look and increases the distance between them.

Dudley Well, Dicker . . . one thing that has always been a great mystery to me is the exact age of the Almighty. How old is God?

Jon Good, good. Good God. Well, Dudley, it isn't really a question of age with God. You see, God is ageless. That is to say he's age old. He's old aged, if you like. In fact, God is as old as he feels and that's the message I'm trying to get across to you youngsters down at my little dockland parish of St Jack in the Lifeboat. You see, I think we have to get right away from this stuffy old idea of thinking of God as something holy or divine, and once we do that we'll get you youngsters flooding back into the churches – I

---

* For music see pp. 152–153.

know that for sure. Now, Alan – is there anything in the Bible that puts you off religion?

Alan ⎱ (*together*) ⎰ Well, I'm glad you asked me that.
Dudley ⎰   ⎱ Thank you, Alan, do you mind, do you mind . . .

Dudley   Thank you Alan – can we leave Lot's wife till later? Well, Dicker, during my study of the good work I was very shocked by all the cruelty and violence in the New Testament. I mean, take for example this ghastly case of shoving a needle up the eye of a camel. Now that's taking unfair advantage of a dumb animal. It's an appalling sight, the poor old ship of the desert standing there with a needle in his eye – and frankly, Dicker, that was the straw that broke the camel's back.

All   Last straw.

Jon   Yes, thank you, yes, well, I think you are putting words into God's mouth here, and I think we can turn a blind eye on the whole affair – after all, the camel had to, by Jove, yes. But I am very grateful to you, Dudley, for bringing this up, because it does bring me to the whole problem of juvenile violence in general. Now I think an awful lot of tommyrot has been spoken about teenage and juvenile violence – I think we can use this violence and channel it towards God. It is my aim to get the violence off the streets and into the churches where it belongs. In the old days, people used to think of the saints as pious old milksops – well, they weren't. The old saints were rough, toothless – no, I mean tough, ruthless tearaways who knew where they were going. Matthew, Mark, Luke and John went through life with their heads screwed on. That's the little rhyme we all sing – and with these principles firmly in mind, we've now got ourselves a young vigorous church where youngsters like yourselves can come in off the streets, pick up a chick, jive in the aisles, and really have yourselves a ball. The result is we are playing to packed houses every night, except of course for Sunday, when we are forced to close our doors because of the Lord's Day Observance Society.

Let's Face It
Alan Bennett solo

Settle down. Come on, now, settle down. That's better. What
do you believe in . . . most? Or *are* you the believing sort? Lot
of people aren't, you know. Meet an awful lot of disillusioned
beggars about these days. They're so bored, so bloody bored.
Can't say I've got much patience with them myself. But then,
me, I *am* the believing sort. And you ask me what I believe in
. . . well, it's this. You be nice to people, people'll be nice to
you. Nothing ethical or philosophical about it. Just good
straightforward common sense. And, my goodness, don't we
need that sort of common sense in the world today.

Now, I'm not a thinking man – and I wouldn't like you to
think that I was – but I don't mind saying I've knocked about
a bit in the world, more than most people get the chance to, I
suppose. And I don't mind saying I'm thankful for it. And do
you know what seems to me to be the fundamental problem
in the world today? It's people. They're so intolerant.

Of course, when I say 'people', I don't mean the ordinary
working sort of chap. I mean, he's happy enough with the
little woman at home, pottering about the garden with his
flutter on the pools at the weekend. He's happy enough with
that . . . and thank goodness for it. That's what *I* say. Where
would we be today without the British Working Man?
Nowhere at all, nowhere at all.

No, the people I mean are these so-called intellectuals.
The kind of chap who mugs up a lot of books, gets hold of a
lot of useless knowledge about what people are like, and then
starts meddling in everything. Let me tell you something I've
learned as I've gone through life. It's this. The lessons of this
life – the really important lessons, that is – are learned, not
from books, but from people. That's why I've never bothered
much with reading. And that's the trouble with these
intellectuals – they've no idea what people are like, and so
they're intolerant.

Take foreign policy. Now, you know, I'm not sure – I'm
not sure, you know, if we weren't just a little bit *nicer* to these
Russians things might not be just a little easier internationally
speaking. I mean, there's nothing wrong with Mr Khruschev
as far as I can see. He's a bit . . . a bit bluff, he's a bit of a

rough diamond, but his heart's in the right place. And that's what matters. And I know I'm leaving myself wide open when I say this – but, you know, some of these Communists are nice chaps. And a damned sight easier to talk to than some of these Labour johnnies in parliament. I mean, let's face it, these Communists are *in* the world. They're *here*. They compose three-fifths of the world's population. Three-fifths . . . that's including the Chinks, of course. Three-fifths. Makes you think, doesn't it. We can't do anything about it, so the sooner we roll up our sleeves and get down to the business of learning to live with them the better it'll be for all concerned. Mind you, I'm not saying they're as good as we are. *I* know they're not, and *you* know they're not, and nothing any of these intellectual blighters says is going to convince me otherwise. But, you know, that's not the point. When you want to borrow your next-door neighbour's lawn-mower, you don't first of all make sure he changes his underpants twice a week, do you? Of course not. It's just the same in politics.

And take all this business about South Africa. These people . . . and it's the same people, these intellectual blighters, just because there's some minor aspect of the internal policy of the legally elected government of South Africa that they don't agree with . . . when, mind you, they've absolutely no acquaintance with the circumstances involved, none at all . . . they think that by not eating pineapples they're going to improve the situation. Mind you, I've been to South Africa, I've met and talked to some of the Afrikaaners, and, let me tell you, they're jolly nice people. Jolly nice. And I'm proud, yes, proud, to call some of them my friends. And what's more, they believe in what they're doing and are prepared to make sacrifices to achieve it. That, by the way, is something else I've learned as I've gone through life. The best things in life, the really best things (which, is, after all, what the South Africans are striving after) aren't achieved without a good deal of hardship, without great heartsearching, possibly . . . yes even without bloodshed. What, after all, did two world wars teach us if it didn't teach us that? So jolly good luck to the South Africans. That's what *I* say.

It all boils down to this, doesn't it: let's keep a sense of proportion. Don't go to extremes, and, above all, don't let's take any notice of these demonstrators, because they're all the same – same crowd, same lot – these people who boycott pineapples and these who go traipsing about the country with their banners and their jazz bands against hydrogen bombs. After all, let's face it, this is a democracy. Government isn't run by people like that, it's run by the people. And don't you go away with the idea that I've not thought about the hydrogen bomb. I have. I've thought about it a great deal. I know it kills millions of people. I know it seals the fate of millions as yet unborn. I know this. All right, fair enough. But I put this to you – the hydrogen bomb is just the same as the bow and arrow . . . in principle. And thank God there are still some of us in the modern world who care about principles. Good night.

5: Bollard

Alan on the rostrum with a cine camera. Enter Jon and Peter with sou'-westers.

Jon   So I said to him, I said, do you do vests in mauve? And he said, no we do not do vests in mauve. And I said, don't do vests in mauve? And he said no, so I had to settle for the green, the Lincoln green.

Peter   Never mind, I think you look lovely in green – it shows off your tanned navel.

Jon   Hello, Arthur, what have we got today?

Alan   Bollard.

Jon   Bollard – that sounds exciting – what is it, a girdle?

Alan   (*sourly*) No, it's a cigarette.

Peter   Someone got out of bed the wrong side this morning, didn't they.

Dudley enters with sou'-wester.

Dudley Hello, men! So sorry I'm late, I got held up at the hairdressers. I was so worried about it, I can't tell you. He was going on and on and I said, 'Stop, you'll *ruin* it!'

Jon   No, he hasn't.

Dudley What's the back like?

Peter   Lovely, lovely – you can scarcely see the join.

Dudley Oh, *thank* you, very nice. (*Bumps into Jon*) Oh, hello – I say, have you seen what I've seen? Clasp your eyes on that then – what a *lovely* tie!

Peter   It *is* a lovely tie. It's the new colour.

Dudley What's that?

Peter   Blue. Can't you see?

Dudley Where did you get it?

Peter   'Homique'. I picked it up for a song.

Dudley And a dance – ooh! I say – aren't these sou'-westers *fabulous*!

Alan   Come along, then.

They put on the sou'-westers and form into a group. Alan puts out a hand to move Dudley.

Dudley Oh, please don't touch me this morning, Arthur, I'm feeling so *fragile*.

Peter   (*adjusting his hair*) Just a moment, I've got a wisp out.
Dudley Have you really?
Peter   Just a wisp, yes.
Alan   (*operating the camera*) Are you ready then? – Right – Action!
Dudley, Peter & Jon (*singing tune: 'Sailor's Hornpipe'*)
                    Stormy days at sea are followed
                    By the smoking of a Bollard
                    Once that lovely smoke is swallowed
                    So much satisfaction.
Jon   Smoke Bollard – a *man's* cigarette.
All   Whoops!

6:   The Heat-Death of the Universe

Jonathan Miller solo

Some years ago, when I was rather hard up, I wanted to buy myself a new pair of trousers – but, being rather hard up, I was quite unable to buy myself a *new* pair. Until some very kind friend whispered into my earhole that if I looked sharp about it I could get myself quite a nice secondhand pair from the sales department of the London Passenger Transport Board Lost Property. Now before I accepted this interesting offer I got involved in a great deal of fastidious struggling with my inner soul, because I wasn't very keen to assume the trousers which some lunatic had taken off on a train going eastbound towards Whitechapel.

However, after a great deal of moral contortion, I steeled myself to the alien crutch, and made my way towards the London Passenger Transport Board Lost Property Sales Department in Portman Square, praying as I did so, 'Oh God, let them be dry-cleaned when I get there.' And when I arrived there, you can imagine my pleasure and surprise when I found, instead of a tumbled heap of lunatics' trousers, a very neat heap of brand new, bright blue corduroy trousers. There were *four hundred* of them! How can anyone lose four hundred pairs of trousers on a train? I mean, it's hard enough to lose a brown paper bag full of old orange peel when you really want to. And anyway, four hundred men wearing no trousers would attract some sort of attention. No, it's clearly part of a complex economic scheme on the part of the London Passenger Transport Board – a complex economic scheme along Galbraithian or Keynesian lines, presumably. So over now to the Economics Planning Division of the London Passenger Transport Board Ops room:

'All right, men. Operation Cerulian Trouser. Now we are going to issue each one of you men with a brand new, bright blue pair of corduroy trousers. Your job will be to disperse to all parts of London, to empty railway carriages, and there to divest yourselves of these garments and leave them in horrid little heaps on the floors of the carriages concerned. Once the trousers have left your body, your job ends there, *and I mean that!* All right, now – are there any questions? Good – now, chins up – and trousers down!'

And they disperse to places far out on the reaches of the
Central Line – places with unlikely names like Chipping
On-gar – places presumably out on the Essex marshes, totally
uninhabited except for a few rather rangy marsh birds
mournfully pacing the primeval slime.

And there in the empty railway carriages they let
themselves separately and individually into the empty
compartments; and then, before they commit the final
existential act of detrouserment, they do those little personal
things which people sometimes do when they think they're
alone in railway carriages. Things like . . . things like smelling
their own armpits.

It's all part of the human condition, I suppose. Anyway, it's
quite possible they didn't even take their trousers off in the
compartments but made their way along the narrow corridor
towards the lavatory at the end – that wonderful little room,
where there's that marvellous unpunctuated motto over the
lavatory saying, 'Gentlemen lift the seat'. What exactly does
this mean? Is it a sociological description – a definition of a
gentleman which I can either take or leave? Or perhaps it's a
Loyal Toast? It could be a blunt military order . . . or an
invitation to upper-class larceny . . . but anyway, willy-nilly,
they strip stark naked; and then, nude – entirely nude – nude
that is except for cellular underwear (for man is born free but
everywhere is in cellular underwear) they make their way back
to Headquarters through the chilly nocturnal streets of
sleeping Whitechapel – 400 fleet white figures in the night –
their 800 horny feet pattering on the pavements and arousing
small children from their slumbers in upstairs bedrooms.
Children who are soothed back into their sleep by their
parents with the ancient words: 'Turn your face to the wall,
my darling, while the gentlemen trot by.'

7:   Deutscher Chansons

Jon   And now Dudley Moore accompanies himself upon the
pianoforte in settings of European songs. First a setting by
Fauré of Verlaine's poem, 'La nuit s'épanouit', in which the
poet bemoans the evil spirits which are at the bottom of his
garden. 'La nuit s'épanouit'.

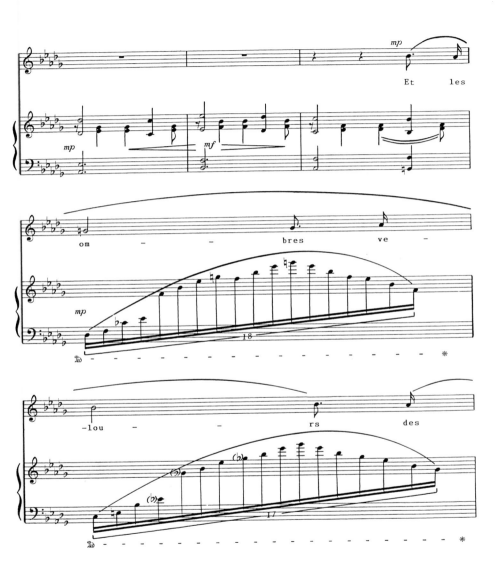

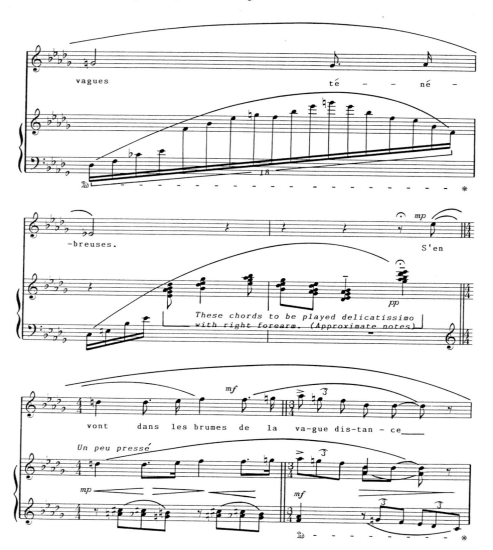

Jon And now Dudley Moore continues to play with himself, this
time in a setting by Schubert of Schiller's poem, 'Die
Flabbergast', in which the poet and his lover bemoan, and
bemoan, and bemoan. 'Die Flabbergast.'

*The song is sung by one voice, alternating between tenor and soprano
range as in a duet. The words are mainly gibberish and may be
altered to suit the convenience of the singer, who may find certain
sounds easier to sing than others especially on the high soprano notes
and during passages of quick alternation between tenor and soprano.
The only words that should be unchanged are 'Die Flabbergast'.*

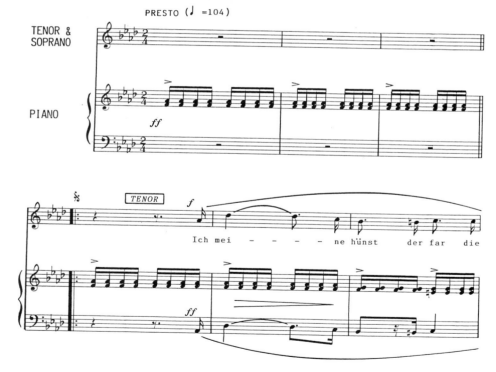

fla-bber-gast   und   swein — — — — — hünst   die

fein   hein   heinst.

staccato

8:   The Sadder and Wiser Beaver

Alan   And you're still working for Beaverbrook?

Peter   Well, yes, I'm still working for the Beaver, if work's the right word; don't get me wrong, Alan – I haven't changed, working on the paper hasn't altered my outlook. You and I in the old days used to think alike on most things – well, it's just the same now: you name any issue and I'll agree with you on it.

Just because my name's at the top of the column you mustn't think that I have any connection with it. It's just that I *like* Mountbatten, and if ever I have to write anything on him – every now and then I am forced to write something – I always ring him up and apologise, or get my secretary to. You've met the wife – got a lovely little house now down in East Grinstead, two little kids: you've got to fight for it, haven't you. We go for holidays in Germany to make up for it, drink a stein with the people – I like the people.

I'm working on the novel, you know. One day that novel's going to come out and blast the lid off the whole filthy business – name the names, show up Fleet Street for what it really is – a really accurate novel about all those people. Of course, if you are going to write a really *accurate* novel, you've got to join the people you are writing about – for a period, anyway. I am going through a sort of research period at the moment. There are about ten of us on the paper – young, progressive liberal people who don't believe a word we are writing. I'll tell you what we do – whenever the old man has a party – a cocktail party – we all gather together down the far end of the room, and we drink as much as we can – we really knock it back – we drink and drink and drink – we're trying to break him from within. And do you know what we do then – quite openly, behind our hands, we snigger at him.

Alan   You snigger at him?

Peter   That's right. We snigger and titter at the Beaver – we go, 'Ha ha, putting on a bit of weight in St Tropez.'

Alan   Well, I don't know – it doesn't seem very much to me, sniggering and tittering.

Peter   A titter here, a titter there – it all adds up – you'd be surprised.

Alan   Take me – I'm no saint, but I turned down five thousand a year with an advertising agency, because I didn't want to make that sort of money.

Peter   Yes, I think that is wonderful of you Alan, really wonderful – in a way I wish I could be like you. But we don't all come into fifty thousand pounds at the age of twenty-one.

9:   Words . . . and Things

Jon and Alan enter from opposite sides.

Alan   Hello there, Urchfont, how are you?
Jon   Hello there, Bleaney.
Alan   Hello . . . what was that little philosophical paper you were telling me about in Common Room – 'Hegel's Moral Doubts' I think you said it was?
Jon   Oh, that – well, it's not really a paper so much as an annotation which I've run up for the proceedings of the Aristotelean Society. It's certainly no *Principia* – shall I fire ahead?

Dudley walks on and then goes off.

Alan   Oh, yes.
Jon   Now, Wittgenstein says, does he not – rather ham-handedly in my opinion – in the Blue and Brown books, that the statement, 'fetch me that slab' implies there *is* a slab, such that were I to fetch it, the statement 'fetch me that slab' would be disjunctively denied by the opposite statement.
Alan   Yes.
Jon   Well, it seems to me that Wittgenstein has made rather a bad blunder here, for as far as I can see the unfetched slab can claim to exist really no more than the unseen tree in the quad.
Alan   No, no – I think you're making a rather primitive category mistake here.
Jon   Surely not.
Alan   Oh no, you're not, it's me. I'm terribly sorry.
Jon   No, no, no – it seems to me that what we have here is an example of a synthetic *a priori* proposition of the sort, 'there are are no sense data which are *both* blue and green all over at the same time *and* sense data', which is a statement really both about our world as we know it in the Wittgenstein sense of everything that is the case, and also a statement about our language as we use it. Now I know you get very worked up about propositional disjunctive functions, Bleaney, so I thought you might like to deal with the whole . . .
Alan   Yes.

Jon	I see . . . well, tell me, are you using 'yes' in its affirmative sense here?
Alan	No, no. I liked that paper. I liked it, you see, because it bears on something I am considering myself, namely what part – what *role* we as philosophers play in this great heterogenous, confusing and confused jumble of political, social and economic relationships we call Society. I mean, other people have *jobs* to do, don't they – what do people do these days? . . .
Jon	They chop down trees.
Alan	*They* chop down trees, they drive buses or they play games.
Jon	Yes, that's very important – they *play* games.
Alan	Now, *we* also play games, but we as philosophers play *language* games. Games of language. Now, when you and I go onto the cricket pitch, we do so secure in the knowledge that a game of cricket is in the offing. But when we play language games we do so rather in order to find out what game it is we are playing. In other words, why do we do philosophy at all? Why?
Jon	Why yes, why yes . . . no, no. I think I must take exception with you on that point, Bleaney, for it seems we want to ask not so much *why* questions as *how* questions.
Alan	Why?
Jon	Well, there you are – need I say more?
Alan	Yes.
Jon	Well, I shall. It seems to me that philosophers – or at least they like to *call* themselves philosophers – who start off by asking 'why' questions end up by making pseudo-statements of the sort . . . 'Saturday got into bed with me.'
Alan	Is that a pseudo-statement?
Jon	Well, I'll take one from real life in that case to hammer home the point . . . 'There is too much Tuesday in my beetroot salad', or something of that general sort.
Alan	I think that is perfectly obvious, but I don't think you are saying – and I don't think you *would* say, would you – that these statements are in themselves meaningless.
Jon	Oh, good heavens, no. All I am saying, really, is that such statements are in themselves metaphysical statements.
Alan	Metaphysical statements? Ah well, if they are metaphysical statements I do not think we should forget – or I don't think *you* should forget – as Bradley pointed out, that a man who

	rejects the existence of metaphysics is simply a metaphysician with a rival theory of his own. Oh dear, oh dear, oh dear.
Jon	Yes, yes . . . ouch! In that case, allow me to illustrate with an example from real life.
Alan	You seem very fond of real life.
Jon	Well, yes. Say we meet a friend, say at the factory, or in the pub, or at a football match – we don't say to that friend, do we, '*Why* are you?' . . . it would be quite absurd to say '*Why* are you?' – no, we say, '*How* are you?'.
Alan	So we do. In this connection, what do you think of Plato and Aristotle and C. S. Lewis?
Jon	Well, it seems to me that while Plato and Aristotle and C. S. Lewis – by the way, how is he?
Alan	Oh, he's quite well.
Jon	Oh, I am glad. Now it seems to me that while they had very interesting things to say about the society which they represent. . .
Alan	He's been having a bit of bother with his teeth. They're not what they were.
Jon	Oh, poor fellow.
Alan	In fact they're not *where* they were. They're out. It's a great loss to scholarship.
Jon	Oh, I am sorry to hear that. But as I was saying, while these people –
Alan	What people?
Jon	Plato, Aristotle and poor old toothless Lewis – were asking questions about life and death which are therefore entirely irrelevant . . .
Alan	I call them not philosophers but para-philosophers.
Jon	Para-philosophers . . . how come para-philosophers?
Alan	Well, you've heard of these chaps – paratroopers – well, para-philosophers are the same, you see. Philosophers with their feet off the ground.
Jon	Yes, yes, very saucy. In that case, the burden is fair and square on your shoulders to explain to me the exact relevance philosophy *does* have to everyday life.
Alan	Yes, I can do this quite easily. This morning I went into a shop, and a shop assistant was having an argument with a customer. The shop assistant said 'yes' – 'yes', you see – and

the customer said 'What do you mean, "yes"?' – and the shop assistant said, 'I mean "yes".'

Jon   This is very exciting indeed.

Alan   Here is a splendid example in everyday life where two very ordinary people are asking each other what are in essence philosophical questions – 'What do you mean, "yes"?' – 'I mean "yes"' – and where I, as a philosopher, could help them.

Jon   And did you?

Alan   Well no – they were in rather a hurry . . .

10: T.V.P.M.

Peter Cook solo

Peter stands beside a table on which is a globe. From time to time he points to the globe to illustrate the talk.

Good evening. I have recently been travelling round the world – on your behalf, and at your expense – visiting some of the chaps with whom I hope to be shaping your future. I went first to Germany, and there I spoke with the German Foreign Minister, Herr . . . Herr and there, and we exchanged many frank words in our respective languages; so precious little came of that in the way of understanding. I would, however, emphasise that the little that did come of it was indeed truly precious.

I then went on to America, and there I had talks with the young, vigorous President of that great country, and danced with his very lovely lady wife. We talked of many things, including Great Britain's position in the world as some kind of honest broker. I agreed with him, when he said that no nation could be more honest; and he agreed with me, when I chaffed him and said that no nation could be broker . . . This type of genial, statesmanlike humour often went on late into the night.

Our talks ranged over a wide variety of subjects including that of the Skybolt Missile programme. And after a great deal of good-natured give and take I decided on behalf of Great Britain to accept Polaris in the place of Skybolt. This is a good solution because, as far as I can see, the Polaris starts where the Skybolt left off. In the sea.

I was privileged to see some actual photographs of this weapon. The President was kind enough to show me actual photographs of this missile, beautiful photographs taken by Karsch of Ottowa. A very handsome weapon, we shall be very proud to have them – the photographs that is, we don't get the missile till around 1970 – in the meantime we shall just have to keep our fingers crossed, sit very quietly and try not to alienate anyone.

That is not to say that we do not have our own Nuclear Striking Force – we do, we have the Blue Steel; a very effective missile, as it has a range of one hundred and fifty miles, which means that we can just about get Paris – and, by God, we will.

While I was abroad, I was very moved to receive letters from people in acute distress all over the country. And one in particular from an old-age-pensioner in Fife is indelibly printed on my memory. (*He takes out a letter.*) Let me read it to you. It reads, 'Dear Prime Minister, I am an old-age-pensioner in Fife, living on a fixed income of some two pounds, seven shillings a week. This is not enough. What do you of the Conservative Party propose to do about it?' (*He tears up the letter.*) Well, let me say right away, Mrs McFarlane – as one Scottish old-age-pensioner to another – be of good cheer. There are many people in this country today who are far worse off than yourself. And it is the policy of the Conservative Party to see that this position is maintained.

And now I see the sands of time are alas drawing all too rapidly to a close, so I leave you with that grand old Celtic saying that is so popular up there: goodnight, and may God be wi' ye . . . ee . . .

11: And The Same To You

Dudley Moore piano solo

a.) Quick shocked bounce off stool and down again.
b.) Desperate search for right keys to play.
c.) Leap off stool to face audience terrorised and frozen with yelp of relief.

12: Aftermyth of War

Dudley plays background music on the piano where indicated, beginning with Beethoven's Fifth Symphony opening, followed by 'Top Hat, White Tie and Tails'.

Peter   So you want to know about the war! The thirties were just coming to an end. Heavy with menace the forties were just around the corner. At the Victoria Palace, Lupino Lane was entrancing London with 'Me And My Girl'. At Ascot a year of Royal victories. Walt Disney had done it again with 'Snow White and the Seven Dwarfs'.

Jon   But underneath the gaiety, the storm clouds were gathering. Across Europe, German soldiers were dancing the hideous gavotte of war.

Piano: 'Deutschland Ueber Alles'. Peter and Alan do Nazi salute and marching.

Alan   And then came a break in the clouds.

Jon enters with a paper bag; the others wave.

Jon   I have here from Herr Hitler a piece of paper. (*He bursts the bag; this is echoed by sound effects into a bombing raid*)

Piano: Mozart Sonata under next speech.

Alan   (*putting a headscarf on*) I'll always remember that weekend war broke out. I was at a house party at Cliveden with the Astors and we sat around listening to the moving broadcast by Mr Churchill, or Mr Chamberlain, as he then was. I remember turning to my husband and saying, 'Squiffy, *où sont les neiges d'antan?*' But I did not feel then that all was quite lost and immediately afterwards I got on the telephone to Berlin to try to speak to Herr Hitler, who had been so kind to us on our last visit to Germany that summer. Unfortunately the line was engaged. There was nothing I could do to avert the carnage of the next six years.

Sound of an explosion.

Dudley   Mr Charles Spedding of Hoxton remembers:

Peter   (*coming up through a trap-door*) I'll never forget that day that war was declared. I was out in the garden at the time, planting out some chrysanths. It was a grand year for chrysanths, 1939, I had some lovely blooms. My wife came out to me in the garden and told me of the Prime Minister's announcement of the outbreak of the war. 'Never mind, my dear,' I said to her, 'you put the kettle on and we'll have a nice cup of tea.' (*Disappears through trap*)

Piano: a few bars of 'Run, Rabbit Run'. Sound of an air-raid siren.

Dudley (*shouts*) Put out that light! . . . All over Britain, the humble little people showed the same spirit of courage.

Sound of an air-raid. Jon enters with tea-trolley.

Jon   You could always tell the difference between theirs and ours. Ours had a steady sort of reliable British hum, rather like a homely old bumblebee. Theirs, on the other hand, had a nasty intermittent whine rather like a ghastly foreign mosquito.

Alan   (*off, over the microphone*) Meanwhile, as invasion threatened, England was blanketed in security.

Enter Peter and Dudley with a signpost.

Peter Wait a moment now. We'll put Ipswich round there.

Dudley We'll put Lyme Regis where Ipswich was.

Peter And we'll put Great Yarmouth where Lyme Regis was. There, now, that should fool the Boche. Bye-bye then. Here . . . how do we get home?

Jon   Home. The very word had a sort of comforting sound, didn't it? Homes whose very foundations were built upon the air. Young men, scarcely boys, tossed aside youthful things and grew up overnight in the grimmer game that is war. A game where only one side was playing the game. Young men flocked to join the Few.

Dudley Please, sir, I want to join the Few.

Jon   I'm sorry, there are far too many.

Piano: 'I Vow To Thee My Country'.

Peter From the rugby fields into the air.

Jon   From the squash courts into the clouds.

Alan   From the skiffs into the Spitfires.

Jon   This was war.

Piano: Chopin prelude under next speech.

Alan   I had a pretty quiet war, really. I was one of the Few. We were stationed down at Biggin Hill. One Sunday we got word that Jerry was coming in – over Hastings, I think it was. We got up there as quickly as we could, and everything was very calm and peaceful. England lay like a green carpet below me, and the war seemed worlds away. I could see Tunbridge Wells, and the sun glinting on the river, and I remembered that last weekend I'd spent there with Celia that summer of '39, and her playing the piano in the cool of the evening. Suddenly, Jerry was coming at me out of a bank of cloud. I let him have it, and I think I must have got him in the wing, because he spiralled past me out of control. As he did so – I will always remember this – I got a glimpse of his face, and, you know – he smiled. Funny thing, war.

There is the sound of hearty singing with the piano: 'Let Him Go, Let Him Tarry' etc. Peter enters.

Peter   Perkins! (*Jon breaks away from the singing*) Sorry to drag you away from the fun, old boy. War's not going very well, you know.

Jon   Oh my God!

Peter   We are two down, and the ball's in the enemy court. War is a psychological thing, Perkins, rather like a game of football. You know how in a game of football ten men often play better than eleven – ?

Jon   Yes, sir.

Peter   Perkins, we are asking you to be that one man. I want you to lay down your life, Perkins. We need a futile gesture at this stage. It will raise the whole tone of the war. Get up in a crate, Perkins, pop over to Bremen, take a shufti, don't come back. Goodbye, Perkins. God, I wish I was going too.

Jon   Goodbye, sir – or is it – *au revoir?*

Peter   *No*, Perkins.

Jon goes off.

Alan But London, that gallant old lady, nurtured her children well.
Dudley At the National Gallery, in a series of lunchtime concerts,
Dame Myra Hess wove her magic fingers inextricably into the
heartstrings of London.

Piano: 'Moonlight Sonata' mixed up with 'Lili Marlene'.

Jon The music you are listening to, Timothy, is German music. We are fighting the Germans. That is something you are going to have to work out later on.

Sound of gun-shots and air-raid.

Peter (*comes up through the trap-door*) That was the night they got Pithy Street. I'll never forget it. I was out in the garden at the time planting out some deadly nightshade for the Boche. My wife came out to me in the garden and told me the abominable news. 'Thousands have died in Pithy Street,' she said. 'Never you mind the thousands dead,' I said to her, 'you put the kettle on and we'll have a nice cup of tea.' (*Disappears through trap*)

Jon How many children do you have, Andrews?

Alan (*working-class voice*) I got six, sir, how about you, sir?

Jon Mary and I only had twenty-four hours before I came out here. I've never ever seen my son Timothy. We've got him down for Eton, of course. You know – he has the makings of a damn fine football player, Mary tells me.

Alan Good show, sir!

Jon Look Andrews – I've not said this before, but we've been right through this beastly business together, now, right the way through.

Alan So we have, sir.

Jon And until this horrible war started, I'd never known men of your social class before; and there is just one thing I'd like to say, Andrews: it's been a privilege.

Alan God bless you, sir. God bless you.

Jon Right, this is it. Let's go.

They go off.

Dudley How grateful we were to the BBC in those dark days of the war when every night at nine o'clock Alvar Lidell brought us news of fresh disasters.

Jon (*off, over the microphone*) This is Alvar Lidell bringing you news of fresh disasters.

Peter (*enters through the trap-door*) I never used to hear the nine o'clock news because I was always out in the garden round

about nine-ish planting out some carrots for the night fighters.
But I do remember that black day that rationing was imposed –
my wife came out to me in the garden, her face ashen in hue.
'Charlie,' she said, 'rationing has been imposed and all that
that entails.' 'Never mind, my dear,' I said to her, 'You put on
the kettle – we'll have a nice cup of steaming hot water.'
(*Disappears through the trap*)

Alan   (*entering*) But the tide was turning, the wicket was drying out. It
was deuce – advantage Great Britain. Then America and
Russia asked if they could join in, and the whole thing turned
into a free-for-all. And so, unavoidably, came peace, putting an
end to organised war as we knew it.

Flags fly, balloons fall, bells chime. Peter and Jon re-enter.

Peter   Well, we've done our best, now it's up to the youngsters.
Jon   I wonder what they'll make of it.
All   (*singing*) Should auld acquaintance be forgot
                      And never brought to mind
                      Should auld . . . acq..ai..nt . . .

Heads and voices droop. Slow curtain.

INTERVAL

13: Civil War

Alan is sitting behind a table, with Peter and Jon on either side of him. On the table is a large folded paper bag.

Alan Settle down, now. Come on, settle down. I think we're about all here, so let's get off the launching pad.

Jon Hear, hear.

Alan Her Britannic Majesty's Government is very anxious to popularise the notion of Civil Defence. Now the Government's Defence – what for want of a better word I'll call Policy – is based on the concept of the deterrent. Say, what for the purpose of argument I will call, an un-named power should take a nuclear missile and drop it on the United Kingdom, we in the United Kingdom would then take another nuclear missile and drop it on Russ- on the un-named power. This, you see, would deter them from . . . um . . . rather, it would effectually discourage them . . . well, it would jolly well serve them right. Now I have an apology to make to you. Tonight I was going to bring along a hydrogen bomb to show you – we do have one or two that we send round to Women's Institutes – that sort of thing. Unfortunately, the one I had my eye on was being used this evening.

Peter Now a lot of people in this country today tend to think of the whole problem of the hydrogen bomb as being rather above their heads. Nothing could be further from the truth. The issue is a simple one – kill or be killed.

Dudley *(in audience)* Or both! Ha ha.

Peter I beg your pardon.

Dudley I said 'Or both'.

Peter I thought you did. Thank you.

Dudley Thank you.

Peter Thank you.

Dudley Not a bit.

Alan Shut up.

Peter Now, we shall receive four minutes warning of any impending nuclear attack. Some people have said, 'Oh my goodness me – four minutes? – that is not a very long time!' Well, I would remind those doubters that some people in this great country of ours can run a mile in four minutes. Basically, the defence

79

of Great Britain rests in the hands of our Sea-Slugs. If our Sea-Slugs fail to get through, then we shall fall back on our Blue Waters. If our Blue Waters let us down, we've still got good old germ warfare up our sleeves. Thank goodness for that. Now I must admit here that there is a very strong possibility that our Sea-Slugs won't get through. The British Sea-Slug is a ludicrously cumbersome vehicle, depending as it does on a group of highly trained runners carrying it into enemy territory. But the boffins are working on it day and night – thinking of fitting it out with some ingenious device – wings or something along those lines – and turning it into some sort of flying machine, in which case it will be re-named Greased Lightning. I must sit down here, I can feel one of my attacks coming on.

Dudley Hello, panel, I'd like to ask Mr Charles P. Moody a question if I may.

Alan Who?

Dudley Charles P. Moody.

Peter Well go and find him, he's not here.

Dudley That's *you*, isn't it?

Alan This is Mr Weatherburn.

Dudley Are you sure? Where did I get Charles P. Moody from?

Peter Was he on the poster?

Dudley He's on the poster, I think.

Peter Oh, who did the posters?

Alan Miss Venables.

Peter Miss Venables – she's usually very reliable.

Alan Are you possibly at the wrong meeting?

Dudley What's this about?

Peter Civilian Defence – aspects thereof.

Dudley Civilian Defence – I thought this was a geranium rally.

Alan Doubtless Charles P. Moody is at the geranium rally.

Jon Now, this does mean that if we are lucky enough in any future conflict to be the aggressor, we are in a position to inflict a blow of twenty, thirty, or even forty mega-deaths – or to put that in more human terms, forty million dead bodies strewn all about the place here and there. Jolly good. Following this, our Sea-Slugs will then come into their own in a second wave and bring our score up into the seventy or even eighty mega-death bracket, which is practically the maximum score permitted by the Geneva Convention.

Alan Now I can see one or two of you are thinking, now look here, what if one of our American friends makes a boo-boo, presses the wrong button, and sends up one of their missiles by mistake? It could not happen. You see, before they press that button they've got to get on the telephone to number 10 Downing Street, and say, 'Now look, Mr Macmillan, Sir, can I press this button?' And Mr Macmillan will say 'yes' – or 'no' – as the mood takes him.

Dudley Ha ha ha . . . very good.

Alan Now, there is a flaw in this argument.

Dudley Yes, there is.

Alan . . . and I can see one of you seems to have spotted it. What if Mr Macmillan is out? Perfectly simple! Common sense, really – we'd ask Lady Dorothy. Now, at this point I'd like to throw the whole thing over to you. If you're at all worried – or you've got any questions – about Civil Defence, let's hear about them.

Dudley whistles, tries to attract their attention.

Jon (*trying to ignore Dudley*) Question up here I think . . . (*finding that he can't*) . . . oh dear, we'll have to take this one.

Alan Yes.

Dudley Following the nuclear holocaust, could you tell me when normal public services would be resumed?

Jon Very fair question. We have got it in hand, of course. Following Armageddon, we do hope to have normal public services working fairly smoothly pretty soon after the event. Though I feel in all fairness, I ought to point out that it must needs be something in the nature of a skeleton service.

Peter What can we do from a practical point of view in the event of a nuclear attack? Well, the first golden rule to remember about hydrogen warfare is to be *out* of the area where the attack is about to occur – get *right out* of the area, because that's the danger area, where the bombs are dropping. Get right out of it – get right out of it – if you're out of it you're well out of it, if you're in it you're really in it. If you *are* caught in it when the missile explodes, for goodness sake don't move; stand absolutely stock still – not under a tree, of course, that could be extremely dangerous. Now, what about radiation, I hear a strangled cry. Well, there is a lot you can do about radiation as soon as the dust has settled – the best thing you can do is to hold your breath and jump into a brown paper bag. There's nothing like good old brown paper for protecting you.

Alan unfolds the paper bag and helps Peter to put it over his head, until it covers him to the ground.

Peter   Draw it on rather like a shroud. It's perfectly simple – you're very manoeuvrable. You can do anything you like inside your brown paper bag. So that's the rule – the bomb drops, the dust settles, hold your breath, jump into your brown paper bag, and hop along to your local Civil Defence Leader.

Alan   And he will tell you *exactly* what you can do.

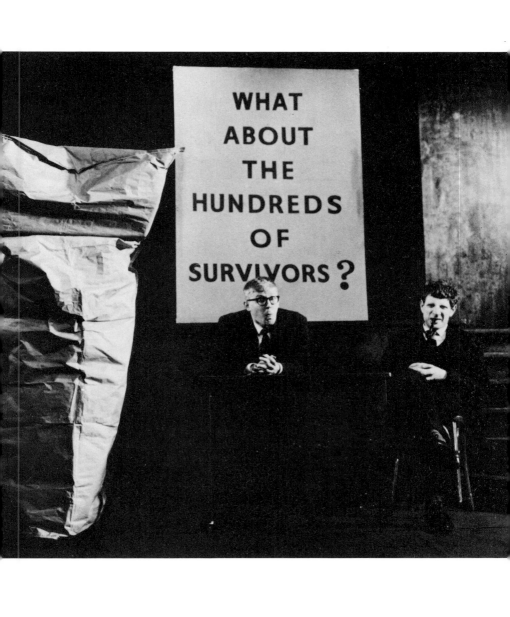

14: Real Class

Peter   I think at about this juncture, it would be wise to point out to those of you who haven't noticed – and God knows it's apparent enough – that Jonathan Miller and myself come from good families and have had the benefits of a Public School education. Whereas the other two members of the cast have worked their way up from working-class origins. And yet Jonathan and I are working together with them in the cast and treating them as equals, and I must say it's proving to be a most worthwhile, enjoyable and stimulating experience for both of us. Wouldn't you agree, Jonathan?

Jon   Oh yes, it certainly is – I'm most impressed by the whole thing.

Alan   Well, I suppose we are working-class. But I wonder how many of these people have realised that Jonathan Miller's a Jew.

Dudley   I suppose he gets away with it because of his ginger hair.

Alan   I'd rather be working-class than be a Jew.

Dudley   Oh, any day. But think of the awful situation if you were working-class *and* a Jew.

Alan   There's always someone worse off than yourself.

Jon   In fact, I'm not really a *Jew*. Just Jew-*ish*. Not the whole hog, you know.

15: Little Miss Britten

Jon Dudley Moore continues to accompany himself on the pianoforte, this time in settings of English songs. A setting by Benjamin Britten of the old English air, 'Little Miss Muffett'. The 'Little Miss Muffett' referred to is thought to have been related to the English entomologist of the same name.

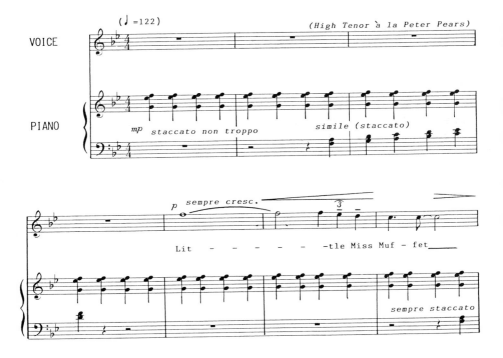

16: The Suspense Is Killing Me

Peter stands upstage with a notice:– 'A Death Cell' – then goes off.
Dudley and Jon sit downstage at a table, playing chess.

Dudley There we are, sir. Your move. Oh, I do believe I've got your
Bishop there.
Jon Is it going to hurt?

Dudley Look, I wouldn't worry about that if I was you, sir. You take a tip from me, I've seen hundreds come and go – relax, let yourself go loose. You're in experienced hands – he's a craftsman, sir.

Jon Is it going to hurt?

Dudley Well, I suppose it's rather like a visit to the dentist. It's always worse in anticipation. But you won't see any of the apparatus, if that's what you're worried about – you'll have a little white bag over your head.

Jon What white bag?

Dudley It's just a little white bag, sir. They make them in Birmingham. But I can't explain to you what goes on out there, I'm not here for that sort of thing, am I now? You wait till the Prison Governor comes down – he'll set your mind at rest. Really he will.

Enter Alan.

Alan Morning . . . and a lovely morning it is too. Though there will be rain before the day is out. Fine before eleven, rain before seven – you know what they say.

Dudley So you'll be missing the rain, sir, won't you?

Alan I don't mind saying, you know, there's been an awful hoo-hah in Parliament about you, and so far as I can see the Home Secretary doesn't like this business any more than you do. But you know what Parliamentary procedure is, and the case being *sub judice* and all that, anyway we'll see if we can't do something about it afterwards. You know, when I was at school I was a bit of a lad, and whenever I used to get into a scrape my headmaster used to say to me, 'Now look here, I'll give you a choice, you can either be gated for a fortnight, or you can take six of the best and we'll forget about it!' Well, like any self-respecting lad I used to take six of the best – what's the difference between this and capital punishment? You don't want to be cooped up for life.

Jon Yes, I do want to be cooped up for life.

Alan Come along, now, you're just playing with words.

Bells start tolling. Jon and Alan go off. Crash, off. Peter enters.

Peter I think it should be done in public.

17: Porn Shop

Jonathan Miller solo

Some years ago, when I was a medical student, I became rather interested in the shops that one finds down the Charing Cross Road in London.
THE SHOPS . . .
where for some curious reason rupture appliances and trusses seem to feature rather prominently.
NOW . . .
I've often wondered to myself why it was that these forms of surgical apparatus did feature in these shops and thought that perhaps it might be some indication of the amount of strenuousness of the life led in the Charing Cross Road and its environs.

I also became interested in the books which they have on sale alongside the trusses in these shops.
NOW . . .
the sort of books I had in mind are not the sort of book that one can look at directly in the windows of the shops concerned.
THEY ARE . . .
the sort of book that one has to glance at *en passant* as one goes down the Charing Cross Road – Hmmmm-HMMMM – !
WELL . . .
I decided to do a sociologial survey on the sort of people that bought these books.
SO . . .
I hacked my way to the back where I found the proprietor of the shop hanging like an ancient orang-utang from one of his own trusses . . . so I tackled him directly.
I SAID . . .
'Now look here who buys all these books which you have on sale in the window here?' and he said, 'Well it's mainly for young married couples wanting to know your wherefore and why.'
AND I SAID . . .
'Well yes I can understand your young married couples wanting to buy books like *Sexual Hygiene in Marriage* but surely your young married couples don't really buy books like a history of flogging in the Army, Navy and Air Force.'

AND HE AGREED WITH ME . . .
that by and large young married couples didn't buy that sort
of book, in bulk at any rate, although a history of the
thumbscrew in the Home Counties had a certain limited sale
which I suppose is understandable.
AND SO . . .
I said, 'Well then who do buy these books?' And he said . . .
'Well I suppose sir you might call them a more mature class
of person sir. Now this mature class of which I glibly speak
falls into what I might best describe as your two broad
cag'atries sir.
TWO VERY BROAD CAG'ATRIES
On the one hand there's your medical students like yourself
. . . After all perversions are in your curriculum aren't they
sir?
AND . . .
On the other hand, by far the largest cag'atry, I'm sorry to say
sir, is your straight warped! It's your straight warped types
what walks in here and asks for books on flogging and the
like . . . and if you want my opinion sir there's only one cure
for that class of warped, distorted mind.'
SO I LEANED FORWARD . . .
anxious to hear of fresh developments in psychotherapy in
this area and he said: 'Yeah, there's only one cure for them
sir. It's a sock in the face and a kick in the arse and whip 'em
to death sir. Yeah, take a whip to them sir. Give 'em a good
dose of their own medicine . . . Yeaaggghhh!'

18: Frank Speaking

Peter This week Studio Five welcomes three distinguished visitors. Now, Mr Taylor, as a member of the Campaign for Nuclear Disarmament, how do you feel about the Labour Party decision to reject nuclear disarmament?

Alan Well, frankly I am a little disappointed, but I know it does not represent the opinion of the rank and file of the Labour Party.

Peter How do you come to this conclusion, Mr Taylor?

Alan All I can say is this: we sent round a referendum to all our local branches phrased in this form – 'Would you like to see your wife and kids go up in smoke?'. Ninety-four per cent of the replies said '*no*'. If that is not a mandate for unilateral nuclear disarmament I do not know what is.

Peter Mr Taylor, thank you. We have with us this evening the newly appointed Lord Chamberlain. Lord Cobbold, what is your opinion of censorship in the theatre?

Dudley Censorship in the theatre. Well, frankly I feel there's far too much sex and violence gets by in the name of entertainment these days. I mean, I go to the theatre to be entertained. I want to be taken out of myself. I don't want to see lust and rape, incest and sodomy – I can get all that at home.

This then goes directly into the next sketch, number 19.

19: Black Equals White

Peter   Also with us this evening we have Mr Akiboto Nobitsu, the leader of the Pan-African Federal Party, who is in London this week for the African Constitutional Conference. Now, Mr Nobitsu, what hopes do you hold out for a successful conclusion to this conference?

Jon   There can be no hope for a successful conclusion to this conference until the fundamental rights of man are realised by the British Government. One man, one vote. That is the law of God which all must obey, including God. One man, one vote, that is essential – especially for the nine million black idiots who vote for me.

Peter   Mr Nobitsu, how do you view the imprisonment of your colleague, Mr Bandabaku?

Jon   The imprisonment of Mr Bandabaku is a most immoral, disgusting and illegal act and definitely not cricket. It is an outrageous and despicable act, and I am in favour of it as it lets me get on with a little bit of agitating on my own.

Peter   Mr Nobitsu, do you in any way condone the violent methods used by your party to further their ends?

Jon   By 'violent methods', Mr Edwards, I presume you are referring to the isolated and sporadic outbreaks of entire communities being wiped out?

Peter   Yes, I did have that in mind.

Jon   Well, all I can say to that is, 'Mote and Beam'.

Peter   I beg your pardon?

Jon   'Mote and beam.'

Peter   Mote and beam?

Jon   'Mote and beam'. Wipe out the mote from your own eye, Great Britain, before you start messing about with our beams. Everywhere the black man is misrepresented. For example, recently I went in London to see this play, *Fings Ain't What They Used To Be*, and in this play there was a black man who was laying around all over the place doing nothing, implying that all black men are layabouts.

Peter   But surely, Mr Nobitsu, you might as well say that the same play implied that all white people were pimps or prostitutes?

Jon   Well, that is fair comment. There can be no progress, Mr Edwards, until you Englishmen stop looking down your noses at us Africans.

Peter (*looking down his nose*) Yes, I *think* I see what you mean . . .

Jon Black equals white, Mr Edwards, no taxation without representation. Black equals white.

Peter Mr Nobitsu, one thing rather puzzles me about you, and that is, your hair is extremely straight, and your complexion seems to be white in colour.

Jon That is perfectly true. I have recently undergone an operation to straighten my hair and also remove the pigmentation from my skin.

Peter Doesn't this rather fly in the face of your principles?

Jon Not at all. I can represent the interests of my people best by speaking to the white man on his own ground. Besides, it is the only way in which I can get lodgings.

Peter Mr Nobitsu, thank you and goodnight . . . There, I think we are safe now. If you would like to go up and join Lord Cobbold and Mr Taylor I'm sure you three must have lots to talk about.

Peter exits. Jon joins Alan and Dudley. They stand in embarrassed silence.

20: Sitting on the Bench
Peter Cook solo

Yes, I could have been a judge but I never had the Latin,
never had the Latin for the judging, I just never had
sufficient of it to get through the rigorous judging exams.
They're noted for their rigour. People come staggering out
saying, 'My God, what a rigorous exam' – and so I became a
miner instead. A coal miner. I managed to get through the
mining exams – they're not very rigorous, they only ask one
question, they say, 'Who are you', and I got 75 per cent on
that.

Of course, it's quite interesting work, getting hold of lumps
of coal all day, it's quite interesting. Because the coal was
made in a very unusual way. You see God blew all the trees
down. He didn't just say 'let's have some coal'. As he could
have done, he had all the right contacts. No, he got this great
wind going you see, and blew down all the trees, then over a
period of three million years he changed it into coal –
gradually, over a period of three million years so it wasn't
noticeable to the average passer-by . . . It was all part of the
scheme, but people at the time did not see it that way. People
under the trees did not say 'Hurrah, coal in three million
years', no, they said 'Oh dear, oh dear, trees falling on us –
that's the last thing we want' and of course their wish was
granted.

I am very interested in the Universe – I am specialising in
the Universe and all that surrounds it. I am studying Nesbitt's
book – *The Universe and All That Surrounds It, an Introduction*.
He tackles the subject boldly, goes through from the
beginning of time right through to the present day, which
according to Nesbitt is October 31, 1940. And he says the
earth is spinning into the sun and we will all be burnt to
death. But he ends the book on a note of hope, he says 'I
hope this will not happen'. But there's not a lot of interest in
this down the mine.

The trouble with it is the people. I am not saying that you
get a load of riff-raff down the mine, I am not saying that. I
am just saying we had a load of riff-raff down *my* mine. Very
boring conversationalists, extremely boring, all they talk about
is what goes on in the mine. Extremely boring. If you were

searching for a word to describe the conversation, 'boring' would spring to your lips – Oh God! They're very boring. If ever you want to hear things like: 'Hallo, I've found a bit of coal.' 'Have you really?' 'Yes, no doubt about it, this black substance is coal all right. Jolly good, the very thing we're looking for.' It's not enough to keep the mind alive, is it.

Whoops. Did you notice I suddenly went 'Whoops'? It's an impediment I got from being down the mine. 'Cause one day I was walking along in the dark when I came across the body of a dead pit pony. 'Whoops' I went in surprise, and ever since then I've been going 'Whoops', and that's another reason I couldn't be a judge, because I might have been up there all regal, sentencing away, 'I sentence you to Whoops' – and you see, the trouble is under English law that would have to stand. So all in all I'd rather have been a judge than a miner.

And what is more, being a miner, as soon as you are too old and tired and sick and stupid to do the job properly, you have to go. Well, the very opposite applies with the judges. So all in all I'd rather have been a judge than a miner.

Because I've always been after the trappings of great luxury, you see, I really, really have. But all I've got hold of are the trappings of great poverty. I've got hold of the wrong load of trappings, and a rotten load of trappings they are too, ones I could've very well done without. (*Looking round suddenly*) Oh, he's gone.

21: Bread Alone

Enter Alan, Dudley, Peter and Jon.

Jon	Very good to see you.
All	Very good to see you . . . nice to see you.
Alan	Unless I'm very much mistaken, there's the bar.
Jon	Magic words, bar, ha ha ha.

They come to centre stage.

All	(*variously*) Here we are and there we are. Ahhh, ahhh. Yes, ye-es.
Alan	Ay, ay, ay.
All	Ay, ay, ay.

Period of noises.

Alan	Funny old world.
All	Funny old world.
Peter	Well, what are you going to have?
All	Let me get this one. My round, I insist, my round! What are you going to have?
Peter	Large whisky.
Jon	Double brandy.
Dudley	Glass of vino tinty.
Alan	Rosé.
All	Right, I'll get this, No, I insist, this one's on me. Drinks are on me. Drinks on me.

General search for money, with noises.

Jon	I've got nothing on me.
All	I'm cleaned out. Haven't got a thing on me. Not a penny.
Dudley	Do they take luncheon vouchers?
Peter	Have you got one?
Dudley	No.
Peter	Well they don't take them unless you actually have one.
Jon	Now where are we going to sit for lunch?
All	I don't mind. I'm quite immaterial. I don't mind.
Peter	This is the only table here.

Period of noises. They move over to the table and chairs, sit at table and pick up four menus.

All	Well let's sit over there.
Jon	Let's get hold of the waiter.
All	Waiter! Waiter!
Jon	I've got one. (*He beckons to an imaginary waiter*) Jolly good. Now what are we going to have?

They all study their menus.

All	Aaahhhhhh.
Peter	It looks jolly good to me.
Jon	I'll have the same as you.
Peter	Same as me, eh – I'll go along with you, Buffy, you know this place best.
Jon	Stop smelling your menu and order, Buffy.
Alan	Buffy, come on.
Dudley	I'm not smelling the menu, I can't see a thing. I think I've got my contact lenses in back to front.
Alan	Try this, Buffy. (*He holds up the menu*)
Dudley	(*reads appetizers*) Oh, I can't decide. I'll follow you, Squiff.
Alan	I decided long ago, I'm having what you're having.
Jon	Good, that's four of the same. Where's he gone? Bloody waiter's cleared off. Go find him, Squiff.
Alan	All right. Waiter! (*He goes off*)
Jon, Peter & Dudley	That's it – gone. Cleared off. Bloody waiter's cleared off. I always come here and it's always the same. Didn't I tell you?

22: Take a Pew

Alan Bennett solo

The 29th verse of the 14th chapter of the book of Genesis:
'But my brother Esau is an hairy man, but I am a smooth
man' – my brother Esau is an hairy man, but *I* am a smooth
man. Perhaps I can paraphrase this, say the same thing in a
different way, by quoting you some words from that grand old
prophet, Nehemiah – Nehemiah 7–16.
And he said unto me, what seest thou
And I said unto him, lo!
I see the children of Bebai
Numbering six hundred and seventy-three
And I see the children of Asgad
Numbering one thousand, four hundred and
    seventy-four.
(*more quickly*) I see the children of Bebai
Numbering six hundred and seventy-three
And I see the children of Asgad
Numbering one thousand, four hundred and
    seventy-four.
There come times in the lives of each and every one of us
when we turn aside from our fellows and seek the solitude
and tranquillity of our own firesides. When we put up our
feet and put on our slippers, and sit and stare into the fire;
and I wonder at such times whether your thoughts turn, as
mine do, to those words I've just read you now. They are very
unique and very special words, words that express as so very
few words do that sense of lack that lies at the very heart of
modern existence. That 'I-don't-quite-know-what-it-is-but-
I'm-not-getting-everything-out-of-life-that-I-should-be-
getting' sort of feeling. But they are more than this, these
words, much much more. They are in a very real sense a
challenge to each and every one of us here tonight. What *is*
that challenge?
As I was on my way here tonight, I arrived at the station,
and by an oversight I happened to go out by the way one is
supposed to come in; and as I was going out an employee of
the railway company hailed me. 'Hey, Jack,' he shouted,
'where do you think you're going?' That at any rate was the
gist of what he said. But, you know, I was grateful to him;

because, you see, he put me in mind of the kind of question I felt I ought to be asking you, here, tonight. Where do you think *you're* going?

Very many years ago, when I was about as old as some of you are now, I went mountain climbing in Scotland with a very dear friend of mine. And there was this mountain, you see, and we decided to climb it. And so, very early one morning, we arose and began to climb. All day we climbed. Up and up and up; higher and higher and higher. Until the valley lay very small below us, and the mists of the evening began to come down, and the sun to set. And when we reached the summit we sat down to watch this magnificent sight of the sun going down behind the mountain. And as he watched, my friend very suddenly and violently vomited.

Some of us think that life's a bit like that, don't we? But it isn't. Life, you know, is rather like opening a tin of sardines. We are all of us looking for the key. And, I wonder, how many of you here tonight have wasted years of your lives looking behind the kitchen dressers of this life for that key. I know I have. Others think they've found the key, don't they? They roll back the lid of the sardine tin of life, they reveal the sardines, the riches of life, therein, and they get them out, they enjoy them. But, you know, there's always a little bit in the corner you can't get out. I wonder – I wonder, is there a little bit in the corner of your life? I know there is in mine.

So, now, I draw to a close. I want you, when you go out into the world, in times of trouble, and sorrow, and hopelessness, and despair, amid the hurly-burly of modern life, if ever you're tempted to say, 'Stuff this for a lark'; I want you, at such times, to cast your minds back to the words of my first text to you tonight. 'But my brother Esau is an hairy man, but *I* am a smooth man.'

23: So That's The Way You Like It

This is played with great vigour at tremendous speed in the modern Shakespeare style. The performers wear various period hats to suit their characters. Enter Peter.

Peter Sustain we now description of a time
When petty lust and overweening tyranny
Offend the ruck of state.
Thus fly we now, as oft with Phoebus did
Fair Asterope, unto proud Flanders Court.
Where is the warlike Warwick
Like to the mole that sat on Hector's brow
Fair set for England, and for war!

Enter Jon and Alan.

Jon And so we bid you welcome to our Court
Fair cousin Albany and you our sweetest Essex.
Take this my hand, and you fair Essex this
And with this bond we'll cry anon
And shout Jack Cock o'London to the foe.
Approach your ears and kindly bend your conscience to my
piece.
Our ruddy scouts to me this hefty news have brought:
The naughty English, expecting now some pregnance in our
plan,
Have with some haughty purpose bent
Aeolis to the service of their sail.
So even now while we to the wanton lute do strut
Is brutish Bolingbroke bent fair upon
Some fickle circumstance.

Alan and Peter Some fickle circumstance.

Jon Get thee to Gloucester, Essex. Do thee to Wessex, Exeter.
Fair Albany to Somerset must eke his route
And Scroop do you to Westmoreland, where shall bold York
Enrouted now for Lancaster with forces of our Uncle Rutland
Enjoin his standard with sweet Norfolk's host.
Fair Sussex, get thee to Warwick's bourne,
And there, with frowning purpose, tell our plan
To Bedford's titled ear, that he shall press

With most insensate speed
And join his warlike effort to bold Dorset's side.
I most royally shall now to bed
To sleep off all the nonsense I've just said.

All go off and re-enter as rude mechanicals.

Jon   Is it botched up then, Master Puke?
Alan   Ay, marry and is, good Master Snot.
Dudley 'Tis said our Master, the Duke, hath contrived some
            naughtiness against his son, the King.
Peter   Ay, and it doth confound our merrymaking.
Jon   What say you, good Master Puke? I am for Lancaster, and
            that's to say for good shoe leather.
Peter   Come speak, good Master Puke, or hath the leather blocked
            up thy tongue?
Dudley Why then go trippingly upon thy laces, good Grit.
Peter   Art leather laces thy undoing?
Dudley They shall undo many a fair boot this day.
All   Come, let's to our rural revel and with our song enchant our
            King.

All go off. Re-enter Alan and Dudley.

Dudley (*sings*) Oh Death his face my shroud hath hid*
                      And Lethe drowned my poor love's soul
                      So flee we now to Pluto's realm
                      And in his arms shall I grow old.
Alan   Wise words in mouth of fools do oft themselves belie. Good
            fool – shall Essex prosper?
Dudley Aye, prosper.
Alan   Say you, prosper, fool?
Dudley Aye, prosper.
Alan   Marry then, methinks we'll prosper. And saying prosper do we
            say to cut the knot which crafty nature hath within our bowels
            lockéd up. But soft, who comes here?

Enter Peter.

Peter   Oh good my Lord, unstop your ear and yet
            Prepare to yield the optic tear to my experience
            Such news I bring as only can crack ope
            The casket of thy soul.
            Not six miles hence
            There grows an oak whose knotty thews
            Engendered in the bosky wood doth raise itself
            Most impudent towards the solstice sun.
            So saying did there die and dying so did say. (*Goes off*)

* For music see p. 151.

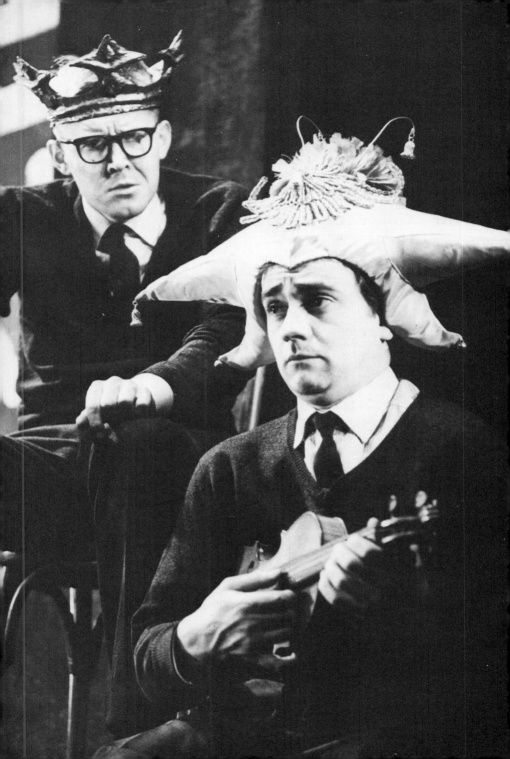

Alan   God! this was most gravely underta'en
And underta'en hath Essex answered it.
Why then we'll muster and to the field of battle go
And unto them our English sinews show.

Goes off. Smoke. Peter and Jon enter with swords.

Jon   Why then was this encounter nobly entertained
And so by steel shall this our contest now be buckled up.
Come sir, let's to it.

Peter   Let's to it.
Good steel, thou shall thyself in himself thyself embowel.

Jon   Come sir.

They fight.

Ah, ha, a hit?

Peter   No, sir, no hit, a miss! Come, sir, art foppish i' the mouth.

Jon   Art more fop in the mouth than fop in the steel.

They fight again. Peter 'hits' Jon.

Oh god, fair cousin, thou hast done me wrong.

Jon goes into protracted death throes, weaving on and off stage.

Now is steel 'twixt gut and bladder interposed.

Finally dies.

Peter   Oh saucy Worcester, dost thou lie so still?

Enter Alan.

Alan   Now hath mortality her tithe collected
And sovereign Albany to the worms his corse committed.
Yet weep we not; this fustian life is short
Let's on to Pontefract to sanctify our court.

24:   The End Of The World

All four sit on the rostrum as if it were a mountain top.

Jon   How will it be, this end of which you have spoken, Brother
             Enim?

All   Yes, how will it be?

Peter   Well, it will be as 'twere a mighty rending in the sky, you see,
             and the mountains shall sink, you see, and the valleys shall
             rise, you see, and great shall be the tumult thereof.

Jon   Will the veil of the temple be rent in twain?

Peter   The veil of the temple *will* be rent in twain about two minutes
             before we see the sign of the manifest flying beast-head in the
             sky.

Alan   And will there be a mighty wind, Brother Enim?

Peter   Certainly there will be a mighty wind, if the word of God is
             anything to go by.

Dudley   And will this wind be so mighty as to lay low the mountains of
             the earth?

Peter   No, it will not be quite as mighty as that, that is why we have
             come *up* on the mountain, you stupid nit – to be safe from it.
             Up here on the mountain we shall be safe. Safe as houses.

Alan   And what will happen to the houses?

Peter   Well, naturally, the houses will be swept away and the tents of
             the ungodly with them and they will all be consumèd by the
             power of the heavens and on earth, and serve them right.

Alan   And shall we be consumed?

Peter   Con-su-mèd? No, we shall not be con-su-mèd. We shall be up
             on the mountain here, you see, while millions burn, having a
             bit of a giggle.

Jon   When will it be, this end of which you have spoken?

All   Aye, when will it be, when will it be?

Peter   Ah, when will it be?

All   Yes, when will it be?

Peter   In about thirty seconds time, according to the ancient
             pyramidic scrolls and my Ingersoll watch.

Jon   Shall we compose ourselves, then?

Peter   Good plan, Brother Pithy. Prepare for the end of the world.
             Fifteen seconds . . .

Alan   Have we got the tinned food?

Dudley Yes.
Peter Ten seconds . . .
Jon And the tin opener?
Dudley Yes.
Peter Five – four – three – two – one – zero!
All (*chanting*) Now is the end – perish the world!

Pause.

Peter It was G.M.T., wasn't it?
Jon Yes.
Peter Well, it's not quite the conflagration I'd been banking on.
Never mind, lads, same time tomorrow – we must get a winner
one day.

Appendices

1. Beyond the Fringe: A Performance History

The term 'revue' has covered a wide variety of theatrical styles since it first emerged in the early years of this century. At first it meant spectacular musical shows – sometimes with a pretence of a plot, sometimes not – in which comedy sketches featuring the same handful of performers in various combinations were interlaced with musical numbers featuring exotic scenery and costumes and as many dancing girls as possible. In the inter-war years the style was stretched to include what were in effect music-hall bills, travelled round as a package under an often irrelevant title; but a major change came during and just after the Second World War, in the form of 'intimate revue'. Here a small cast presented material of a rather more intelligent nature, witty and amusing although rarely indulging in any sort of social or political observation. These shows were still influenced by the older revues to the extent of having musical numbers which often fitted rather unhappily with the sketches.

Amateurs also made use of this format, most notably the members of the Cambridge University Footlights Club, who by the 1950s had established a tradition of a yearly show, given to an audience, which was often of a very high standard (indeed *Out of the Blue* (1954) and *Between The Lines* (1955) played briefly in London's West End). The student revues of this period were witty and lively, and provided the first public appearances of people such as Jonathan Miller, Leslie Bricusse, Joe Melia, Peter Cook and Timothy Birdsall. Oxford, though more inclined towards serious theatrics, had a similar tradition.

It was from this University background that *Beyond The Fringe* was born. An Oxford graduate, John Bassett, was in 1960 assisting Robert Ponsonby, the organiser of the Edinburgh Festival. This annual theatrical and arts festival traditionally attracted a number of unofficial performances, often of an experimental nature, in what had become known as the 'Fringe'. Ponsonby suggested that the Festival might mount its own late-night revue, in competition with the unofficial performances; Bassett suggested two amateur performers of his acquaintance – Dudley Moore, from Oxford, and Jonathan Miller, who had been at Cambridge and was by this time a qualified doctor on his first hospital 'house job'. Moore suggested Alan Bennett, and Miller suggested Peter Cook; and so the four met to examine the possibilities.

Despite their initial reservations about the whole exercise, the four agreed to go ahead, and, with Bassett encouraging them, the revue was put together. The title – which none of them liked – was intended to suggest that what they were presenting was beyond the capabilities of the Edinburgh 'Fringe'. The revue, which started at 10.45 pm and ran for about an hour, consisted of a dozen sketches, only half of which eventually turned up (some in substantially altered form) in the London version – these included Alan Bennett's sermon, the Shakespeare skit, 'Royal Box' and 'The End Of The World'. Sketches which disappeared after Edinburgh included a dig at the newly-formed Gala Films chain of cinemas, a satirical look at the process of admitting refugees into the country, and a thoroughly deserved lampoon of the ITV advertising magazine 'Jim's Inn'. Some of the items – the sermon, for example –

had already been performed elsewhere; some, like the Shakespeare sketch, were newly co-written.

Beyond The Fringe opened on 22 August 1960. Although the critics were impressed, the show did not as yet receive much public acclaim. However, its success was great enough for suggestions to be made that it should be brought to London's West End. Peter Cook's agent somehow succeeded in persuading the cast to accept as producer William Donaldson, whose main theatrical experience had consisted of losing a lot of money by trying to bring the 1959 Cambridge Footlights Revue, *The Last Laugh*, to London. The main attraction of Donaldson seems to have been that he was prepared to leave the four of them entirely alone to do what they wanted, instead of attempting to 'improve' the show, as most producers might be expected to do. It took some time for the four to agree, but eventually an expanded version opened for a week in an out-of-town try-out at Cambridge, on 21 April 1961. Only about half the Edinburgh sketches had survived, and a considerable amount of additional material had been written. Some 35 items (some of them 'quickies' or what used to be called 'blackout sketches', and some of them being variants of other sketches) were submitted to the Lord Chamberlain's office for approval (as was required by the theatrical censorship laws until 1968). Only 23 of these eventually made it to London.

Cambridge saw the first appearance of the famous sketches which gave the show its reputation as a satirical landmark – the lampoon of Harold Macmillan and the Civil Defence sketch among them. There were also several sketches which gave the appearance of demanding a certain amount of intellectualism from the audience – in particular 'Words . . . and Things', which had changed from its Edinburgh version in which all four parodied the manner of pompous university philosophy dons to a conversation between Miller and Bennett which mocked the techniques of philosophy. In fact most of the supposed intellectualism and satire boiled down to the audience's having a reasonable knowledge of what was going on in the world round them.

One of the important features of the show was its staging – unlike previous revues, which had always had scenery and costumes, *Beyond The Fringe* had very little in the way of scenery or props – a rostrum, a few stairs, a table, and occasionally the odd hat for the cast, who otherwise wore grey trousers and jackets or jerseys. This helped to give the show much of its 'bite', although the style was not adopted as a deliberately theatrical effect; it was in fact dictated simply by economy.

The critical acclaim and appreciative audiences which the show enjoyed during its week in Cambridge were not repeated during the subsequent week at Brighton. Here the audience seemed to be totally unable to cope with the show, and the sound of seats banging up and people making their way out became commonplace. One member of the audience remembers a gentleman of military bearing standing up during the 'Aftermyth of War' sketch, shaking his fist at the stage, shouting 'You young bounders don't know anything about it', and storming out. (Indeed this sketch caused persistent trouble among people who saw it as mocking those who lost their lives in the war, rather than the sentimentalised 'stiff-upper-lip' attitude of so many British films of the period.)

The bad reception at Brighton so worried the impresario Donald Albery, (whom Donaldson – being himself still financially embarrassed by his failure with *The Last Laugh* – had persuaded into the deal as a means of getting a theatre) that Albery wanted to pull out entirely; but in the end the show was put into the Fortune Theatre, where it was expected to last just long enough to fill a six-week gap before another production went in. It opened on 10 May 1961.

Many of the items seen in Cambridge had been cut, and others altered. 'Words . . . and Things', in particular, had been considerably simplified, with more actual jokes worked into it, and various other less obvious changes had been made. Most of the quickies (some of which were very slight) were cut.

Once again, critical reaction was euphoric. In particular Kenneth Tynan and Bernard Levin wrote ecstatic revues hailing the show as a breakthrough in satire – a label which somewhat irritated the performers, who were simply trying to be as funny as possible and had deep suspicions of anything as polemical as satire.

The impact of the show on the public was considerable. Although the satirical aspect of it can now be seen in better perspective, at the time it seemed the most important part of the show – partly because such things had not been done on the English stage for many years. Thus it paved the way for the so-called 'satire boom' of the early 1960s, which embraced television's *That Was The Week That Was*, Peter Cook's cabaret club 'The Establishment', and – still around as the last ragged survivor of the era – the magazine *Private Eye*.

Originally expected to run for six weeks, the show ran for over a year with the original cast. A substitute cast took over when the four were offered the chance to take the show to America; this version transferred to the Mayfair Theatre in 1964 and ran, with revisions, until September 1966.

Beyond The Fringe opened at the John Golden Theatre, New York, on 27 October 1962. Few concessions were made to American audiences, the cast feeling that the very English-ness of their style was part of the attraction. Peter Cook re-worked his miner monologue, Alan Bennett replaced his monologue with a new one, and Jonathan Miller added his imitation of Bertrand Russell ('Portraits from Memory').

Some of the sketches were expanded – in particular 'Civil War' and 'The End of the World' which now included considerable digressions. Peter Cook and Dudley Moore were beginning to work together, particularly in the occasional disruptive improvisation, showing the first glimmerings of their later very effective teaming in BBC Television's *Not Only . . . But Also* in 1965.

The show was an immediate cult success. The critics were enthusiastic, and Alistair Cooke commented in *The Guardian*, 'In a way their success is a reprise of the old, and most popular, visiting lecturers, who pitied their audience, said so, and made a mint.' Before the show opened, many experienced theatrical producers had predicted that the performers' refusal to adapt even their accents for American ears would cause them to fail; but the American audiences loved every word of it.

This first Broadway version ran for about a year. At the end of it the partnership broke up – amicably, despite the occasional frictions arising out of living and working in each other's pockets for three years. Jonathan Miller left the world of stage performance, but, instead of returning to medicine went first into television, working for *Monitor*, a BBC arts programme, and then into theatrical and operatic direction.

Beyond The Fringe returned to Broadway in a revised version in 1964. Paxton Whitehead joined the cast in Jonathan Miller's place, giving a creditable impression of Miller's manner without slavishly imitating him. Several new sketches were added, including Dudley Moore's scathing impression of a Kurt Weill song and Peter Cook's performance as a particularly dense police inspector being interviewed on the Great Train Robbery. Once again the monologues were re-written – in particular Peter Cook's miner now went off into a long rambling digression about a troupe of naked ladies wandering in the desert, foreshadowing some of the obsessions of the later version of this character, E. L. Wisty, who appeared in the ITV series *On The Braden Beat*.

Beyond The Fringe has passed into legend. The more-or-less constant availability of the original recording has kept some of the material familiar to the public, while the aura of excitement which the original performances of the show generated is still remembered by many. It did indeed have a profound and far-reaching effect. Though there were other factors at work – such as the closure of many theatres during the late 1950s and early 1960s – *Beyond The Fringe* carries most of the responsibility for the demise of 'old-fashioned revue' of the sort described earlier. Almost overnight the genre disappeared; and the most obvious direct successor to *Beyond The Fringe*, the London version of the 1963 Cambridge Footlights Revue, *Cambridge Circus*, rejected the social observation of the earlier show in favour of more absurd and sometimes surrealistic comedy. This show was, of course, the first London appearance of later comedy stars such as Bill Oddie, Tim Brooke-Taylor and John Cleese.

A field in which *Beyond The Fringe* made a more lasting effect was in theatrical censorship – and by extension, in the freedom of speech allowed on television. The Lord Chamberlain's Office had up until then been extremely rigid in its censorship of the theatre, often with idiotic results. What is surprising is that almost all of *Beyond The Fringe* was passed without comment. (The existing copy in the Lord Chamberlain's Archive does not confirm the story about the stage *directions* for 'Bollard' being censored, although Peter Cook remembers it happening – but does show that the Lord Chamberlain stopped the characters calling each other 'love'. Apart from this there seem to have been no complaints.) Very probably the intelligence and wit of the show protected it from complaints which would have been levelled at a less skilful script; but the relaxed standards applied to the show seem to have established a new norm, and certainly encouraged a greater freedom in what might be said on the professional stage.

As far as television was concerned, the immediate outcome of *Beyond The Fringe* (and also Peter Cook's satirical nightclub 'The Establishment') was the series of satirical late-night shows which began with *That Was The Week That Was*, whose new freedom of expression led on – despite many internal disputes at the BBC – to shows such as *Till Death Us Do Part* and *Monty Python's Flying Circus*. (The full story of this generation of comedy is covered in the present writer's book *From Fringe To Flying Circus**.)

Even though these, and subsequent, shows owed little in their direct approach to *Beyond The Fringe*, their observation and the freedom to express their ideas would probably not have been the same without the pioneering work of the original show. The cast were less than happy about being bracketed with the so-called 'satire boom' – an association which clung to them, like an unwelcome aroma, for years; but of course the particular approach of the 'satire boom' meant that 'satire' came to mean throwing insults at the establishment – particularly the government. *Beyond The Fringe* could be said to be satirical in the broader sense of social satire, but only in that its main purpose was to be funny, and intelligent satire was just one of the techniques it used.

Even though many of the targets at which *Beyond The Fringe* aimed have gone or changed, the scripts in this collection show clearly what a truly comic show it was. Few enough shows have ever approached its quality or gained its long-standing reputation.

Roger Wilmut

*Eyre Methuen, 1980.

2. Additional items from the Broadway versions
authors' credits belong to all four except where stated

Broadway
Portraits from Memory (*Miller*)

Broadway 1964
Home Thoughts from Abroad
The English Way of Death (*Bennett*)
The Weill Song (*music: Moore – words: Cook*)
The Great Train Robbery (*Cook*)
The Death of Nelson (*Miller*)
Interviews (Studio Five) (*Cook, Miller*)
Civil War (additional material)

Portraits From Memory
Jonathan Miller solo

Music, faded out under.

In the third of our series, 'Portraits from Memory', Bertrand Russell reminisces about his early days at Cambridge.

One of the advantages of living in Great Court Trinity, I seem to recall, was the fact that one could always pop across at any time of the day or night and trap the then young, and somewhat beautiful, G. E. Moore into a logical falsehood by means of a cunning semantic subterfuge. I recall one occasion with particular vividness. I had popped across and knocked on his door. 'Come in,' he said. I decided to wait awhile in order to test the ethical consistency of his proposition. 'Come in,' he said once again. 'Very well,' I replied, 'if that is in fact truly what you desire.' I opened the door accordingly and went in. Moore was seated by the fire with a basket upon his knee. 'Moore,' I said, 'have you any apples in that basket?' 'No,' he replied, and smiled seraphically as was his wont. I decided to try a different tack. 'Moore,' I said, 'have you then *some* apples in that basket?' 'No,' he replied again, leaving me in a logical cleft stick from which I had but one way out. 'Moore,' I said, 'have you then *apples* in that basket?' 'Yes,' he replied, and from that day forth we remained the closest of friends.

Home Thoughts From Abroad

Jonathan, Peter and Alan are sitting or standing around the stage as the curtain rises. Dudley enters, walks to the piano, sits down and starts to play THE STAR-SPANGLED BANNER. The other three assist him when he falters by humming the tune.

Peter Very good, Buffy, you've almost got it.

Jon By the way, when are you going to America?

Dudley (*rises*) I'm going in the next couple of days, so I thought I better brush up on my 'Star Spangled Banner'.

Alan Well, of course you have to. You have to be able to play it, otherwise they won't give you a visa. They're terribly sticky about that. Toscanini waited for years and years.

Peter Mind you, I can see their point of view. If they didn't have these sort of regulations, any old riff-raff could get in.

Jon They've got a lot of old riff-raff in there already.

Alan Yes, that's the first thing that will strike you.

Dudley What, the riff-raff?

Peter No, the first thing that will strike you about the Americans is that they're not English.

Jon Well, of course they're not English, they're American.

Peter No, what I mean is they're not English. They're not of English stock. You only have to look at their names . . . Lefkowitz, Wagner, Epstein . . . those aren't English names.

Alan They used to be.

Peter No, they never were.

Alan No, what I mean is, they used to be of good English stock – Anglo-Saxon stock.

Jon Puritan stock . . .

Peter Puritan stock, yes . . .

Alan It was the Statue of Liberty that started the rot.

Dudley How was that?

Alan Well, they put up this statue. It's a lovely statue.

All Yes, a lovely statue . . . lovely thing . . . lovely . . .

Alan And then some idealistic Johnny went and inscribed on the bottom all this business about give me your poor, your huddled masses . . . well, people *did*. The huddled masses leapt at the opportunity. They came over in droves . . .

Peter   Bred like rabbits . . .

Jon   Died like flies . . .

Alan   And spread like wildfire. The whole place was swamped.

Dudley Isn't there a very serious colour problem over there?

Peter   Yes, there is, Buffy, but *you* won't have any difficulty. There are a lot of coloured people about, I did notice that.

Alan   I think there is a danger though of seeing the colour problem simply in terms of black and white.

Peter   It's a lot more complicated than that.

Dudley I gather the Negroes are sweeping the country.

Jon   They are. It's one of the few jobs they can get – and very well they do it, too.

All   Yes . . . first class . . . lovely job . . . wonderful sweepers . . .

Dudley What's all this black muslin I hear they're wearing?

Peter   No . . . they're not wearing it – they're joining it. It's a *movement*, rather than a . . . a cloth.

Dudley I see.

Peter   Of course, one thing, Buffy, you will notice about America, and that is they're a very young country – rather like Ghana in that respect.

Jon   Except for the fact that they have inherited our two-party system.

Dudley How does that work?

Jon   Well, they have the Republican Party, which is the equivalent of our Conservative Party – and then they have the Democratic Party, which is the equivalent of our Conservative Party.

Peter   Then there is the liberal element in the shape of people like Javits.

Dudley Are the liberals Democrats or Republicans?

Alan   Yes . . . as is convenient for them.

Dudley Of course, you know the Americans must be frightfully jealous of our Royal Family.

All   Oh, they are . . . can't blame them . . . poor darlings . . .

Alan   Except there is a sense in which Lyndon Johnson is the Queen and Prime Minister all rolled into one.

Dudley One what?

Alan   Exactly! That's the whole dilemma of the American Constitution.

Jon   I think he's doing a very good job, and he is a very cultured man, too.

Peter   Very cultured indeed – when he had Erhardt down at his ranch, he had Van Cliburn playing Beethoven and a choir singing 'Tief in das Herz von Texas'.

Dudley   Simultaneously, I believe.

Alan   I understand he is now thinking of taking steps to federalize the Avant-Garde.

Peter   An exciting concept. Of course, Buffy, one thing you will notice about the Americans, God bless them, and that is, they are terribly naïve about sex.

Dudley   In what way?

Alan   Exactly!

Peter   They're terribly naïve – I mean, they just think of sex in terms of beautiful blonde women with huge breasts and pink skins and blue eyes . . .

All   Pathetic . . . yes, pathetic . . . very adolescent . . . absolutely pathetic . . .

Peter   How do *you* think of sex?

Dudley   I don't – at least, I try not to – otherwise I start thinking of beautiful blonde women with huge breasts and pink skins . . .

All   Pink skins, yes . . . yes . . . pathetic . . . absolutely pathetic . . .

Jon   I'll tell you one thing I do very much admire about Americans, and that is they do have something to believe in. I mean, they really believe in anti-Communism.

Dudley   Oh, God, I wish we had a positive faith like that in England.

Peter   Yes, it does give you something to hold on to, doesn't it?

Dudley   Isn't there a lot of poverty in America?

Dudley   Yes, there is, but luckily it's all been concentrated in the slum areas. It's beautifully done. You'd scarcely notice it.

Jon   Where do you intend to go?

Dudley   I'm going to New York first.

Alan   Well of course, you must remember – New York isn't America.

Dudley   What is it, then?

Alan   Well, New York is New York . . . it's not *America*.

Peter   It's not America. If you want to see America you want to go to the South.

Alan   Well, the South is charming, but it's not *America*.

Jon   You shouldn't miss seeing Washington, but there's a rather Parisian atmosphere about Washington – it's not *America*.

Peter   Like Los Angeles – it's fascinating, but it's not America, any more than, say, San Francisco – and that's not America.

Jon   Of course, the whole West is terribly exciting, but it's not *America*.

Alan   Then of course there's the North – North America – but that's Canada – that's not *America*.

Dudley   Where *is* America?

Alan   Oh . . . the Cape . . .

Jon   Massachusetts . . .

Alan   That's just a little bit of England.

All   *THAT'S* AMERICA!

The English Way of Death

Alan Bennett solo

(*Northern accent*) I'm just having a look at our Florence's *In Memoriam* notice. We have it put in, like, every [*current date*]. Oh, dear, there's a lot of deaths in tonight . . . Fancy, there's five columns of deaths and only seven births. I think folks are thinning out a bit nowadays. I know one thing – when I go, I want to be burnt. Well, I think it's more hygienic. And, besides, there's a lot less palaver about the service up at the crematorium. It only takes ten minutes. I mean, you go in there, like, and you have a bit of music – Handel's Largo or something like that – then the parson says a few words, and then the coffin goes through and you come out. And do you know, there's folks waiting to get in, they're that busy. Mind you, you have to watch that coffin like a hawk if you want to see it go through. They whisk it away ever so quiet – sst – and it's gone. I know – I went up for my Uncle Wilfred's funeral, and I had my eye on it, I were watching it – and I was just turning around to have a word with our Cora – and, b'joves, when I turned back it had gone. I were that mad.

Then, after a few days, when body's been consumed, they'll send the ashes down to the undertakers, and you go and collect them. Mind you, you don't get them *all*, like – you just get a selection . . . it's about a cigar-box full. We went to Shuttleworth's, were undertakers for me Uncle Wilfred. He's a right lugubrious tup is old Shuttleworth. I went along there like, and he says, 'Good morning, Mr Lightowler – have you come for the deceased's remains then?' I says, 'I've come for me Uncle Wilfred's ashes, you sanctimonious old sod, and look sharp about it.' Mind you, you don't know that them ashes you get are *your* ashes. I mean, how *do* you know? You don't. I mean, for all you know it might be a couple of copies of the *Yorkshire Evening Post* that they burn up . . . It's just like everything else, you just have to believe what they tell you.

Then when you've got them, you've got to decide what you're going to do with them. Mrs, Passmore, she had her husband's put in an egg-timer. She says, 'He's never done a stroke of work during his life; I shall right enjoy watching him now.' Mind you, that's a bit unorthodox, like.

There's a lot of folks – there's an increasing percentage of folks like to have their ashes scattered. They're always scattering ashes up on the golf course – they're pleased to have them up there, because it does the grass good. My aunt Maria Alice, she were in St James's at the finish, and I went to see her; and she says. 'Walt,' she says, 'When I go I want to be scattered.' So I says, 'All right.' She says, 'When I go I want to be scattered on the South Shore at Blackpool.' And I says, 'They won't allow that.' And she says, 'When I go I want to be scattered on the South Shore at Blackpool and on August Bank Holiday Monday.' And I says, 'You're bloody mad,' I says, 'there's crowds of folks there at that time of year, and besides,' I says, 'the municipality won't want all them smuts blowing about there – it's a smokeless zone.' But you couldn't argue with her, and in a sense like you can understand because she hadn't had much of a life, my aunt Maria Alice – happiest time she'd had had been on South Shore, and that were where she wanted to be – anyway, we were talking it over like, after she'd gone, and I says, 'Well, I don't want to take them. I just don't fancy it, that's all – it's against regulations.' And my Uncle Norris, he's as bold as brass – he says, 'Come on, put them in a brown paper bag – *I'll* take them.' So he puts ashes in a brown paper bag, like, and buys a day return to Blackpool, August Bank Holiday Monday. He walks up and down along the South Shore spying out the ground like, and he takes this bag out and starts scattering them about – getting rid of them – and there's crowds of folks about – sunbathing and carrying on like. And do you know, nobody takes any notice of him. They thought he were feeding the seagulls.

Sithee, here's *In Memoriams* . . . we have a verse in this year, what with it being ten years since our Florence went. Anyway . . . 'Lightowler, Florence – passed away (*current date, ten years previous*), beloved daughter of Gladys and Walter Lightowler.' Then we have this verse:

       'Down the lanes of memory
       The lights are never dim
       Until the stars forget to shine
       We shall remember . . . her.'

The Weill Song
Dudley Moore solo

Jon   And now Dudley Moore will sing 'The Ballad of Gangster Joe' from the Weill opera *Walnut*. Libretto by Bertolt Brecht.

The Great Train Robbery

Alan   The great train robbery of over three million pounds continues
to baffle the British Police.

Peter   Good evening.

Alan   However, we have here with us in the studio this evening . . .

Peter   Good evening.

Alan	. . . Sir Arthur Gappy, the First Deputy Head of New Scotland Yard, and I'm going to ask him a few questions about the train robbery.
Peter	Good evening.
Alan	Good evening, Sir Arthur.
Peter	Good evening.
Alan	I'm going to ask you a few questions about the train robbery, if I may.
Peter	Good, the very thing we are investigating. I'd like to make one thing quite clear at the outset – when you speak of a train robbery, this in fact involved no loss of train. It's merely what I like to call the *contents* of the train which were pilfered – we haven't lost a train since 1946, I think it was, the year of the great snows, we mislaid a small one. They're very hard to lose, you see, being so bulky – a train is an enormous thing compared for example to a small jewel, a tiny pearl for example might fall off a lady's neck and disappear into the grass, or the gravel, or wherever she was standing – in the sea, even, and disappear underwater – whereas an enormous train, with its huge size, is a totally different kettle of fish . . .
Alan	I think you've made that point rather *well*, Sir Arthur . . . who do you think may have perpetrated this awful crime?
Peter	We believe this to be the work of thieves, and I'll tell you why. The whole pattern is extremely reminiscent of past robberies where we have found thieves to be involved – the tell-tale loss of property, that's one of the signs we look for, the snatching away of the money substances – it all points to thieves.
Alan	So you feel thieves are responsible?
Peter	Good heavens, no! I feel that thieves are totally *ir*responsible. They're a ghastly group of people, snatching your money away from you . . .
Alan	I appreciate that, Sir Arthur, but . . .
Peter	*You* may appreciate it, but most people don't. I'm sorry I can't agree with you. If you appreciate having your money snatched you must be rather an odd fish.
Alan	You misunderstand me, Sir Arthur, but who in your opinion is behind the criminals?
Peter	Well, *we* are, considerably – we don't seem to be able to catch up with the wretches.
Alan	Who do you think is the organising genius behind the crime?
Peter	Of course, now you're asking me who is the organising genius

behind the crime.

Alan You are a man of very acute perception, Sir Arthur.

Peter Well, let me say this – we think it's a mindermast*.

Alan A mindermast?

Peter Yes, a mindermast.

Alan What exactly *is* a mindermast?

Peter Well a mindermast . . . 'mindermast' is the code word we use at Scotland Yard to describe a master-mind. We don't like to use the word 'mastermind' because that depresses the men, to think they're up against that, so we call it a 'mindermast', in a futile endeavour to deceive ourselves.

Alan I see.

Peter But we are using the wonderful equipment known as 'Identikit' – do you know about that?

Alan Yes, that's when you piece together the face of the criminal, isn't it?

Peter Not entirely, no . . . we're only able to piece together the *appearance* of the face of the criminal. Unfortunately we're not able to piece the *face* together – I wish we could. Once you have captured the criminal face the other criminal parts of the body are not hard to find – the criminal body is situated directly beneath the criminal face – joined of course by the criminal neck . . . anyway, through this wonderful system of 'Identikit', we have pieced together an extremely good likeness of the Archbishop of Canterbury.

Alan So His Grace is your number one suspect?

Peter Well, let me put it this way – His Grace is the man we are currently beating the living daylights out of down at the Yard.

Alan And he is still your number one suspect?

Peter No, I'm happy to say that the Archbishop, God bless him, no longer resembles the picture we built up. A change I think for the better – he thinks for the worse.

Alan I see. I believe I'm right in saying that some of the stolen money has been recovered?

Peter Yes, it has.

Alan And what is happening to that?

Peter We're spending it as quickly as we can. It's a short life, but a merry one. Goodnight.

* 'mindermast' pronounced with i as in 'sin'.

The Death Of Lord Nelson
Jonathan Miller solo

One of the strangest episodes in English History was the
death of Horatio Lord Nelson, the admiral of the British
Fleet, who died in the arms of his friend, Captain Hardy. In
1805 at the time of the Battle of Trafalgar, Admiral Lord
Nelson was only half the man he was. (*Falls, as if having one
leg and one arm*) However, his loyal men put him out of
harm's way on the poop deck – where, being in his right
sense and full possession of his faculties, naturally he was
bored. (*Displays idle boredom – turns hat to Napoleonic position*)
But what were his thoughts when first struck by that fateful
musket ball? (*Sound effect of gunshot*) Hardy! And he falls
stricken and is taken down between decks. Between decks?
Now exactly where *is* between decks? A place so incredibly
narrow that it is totally unsuited for the medical examination
of admirals – so narrow that even doctors have to crawl to
their patients on their bellies. (*Crawls along stage*) 'How are
your bowels?' And there, lying between decks, Nelson says his
dying words. But what *were* his dying words? There is some
historical doubt about this. Some people say that Nelson said,
'Kiss me, Hardy', in which case a young cabin-boy would
have been dispatched up on deck to fetch Captain Hardy –
'Admiral's compliments, sir, Captain Hardy, sir, says you're to
come below and kiss him'. But perhaps it wasn't quite as easy
as that. Hardy might not even have been on the flagship at
the time – and would have been called across miles of stormy
seas. 'Ahoy there! Do you have Captain Hardy aboard, there?
Nelson's gone gaga – wants to kiss him!' When Captain
Hardy arrived, green and grumbling after a bilious trip in a
long-boat – and in no condition to kiss anybody – the whole
thing may have been a waste of time because some authorities
say that Nelson never said 'Kiss me Hardy' in the first place,
but 'Kismet, Hardy' – in which case you can imagine
Nelson's surprise . . . (*Slumps against rostrum*) Kismet, Hardy
. . . Hardy . . . get away from me, Hardy, I'm a sick man . . .
Hardy . . . what do you think you're doing, Hardy? . . . Hardy
. . . aaaaaaaaaahhhhhhhh!

Interviews (Studio Five)

Peter   This week Studio Five welcomes three distinguished visitors. Space is very much in our minds these days, and here to talk about space and science in general is Mr Quintin Hogg, the British Minister of Science.

Alan   Good evening.

Peter   Good evening, Mr Hogg. I wonder if you would tell me what Great Britain's plans are for a space probe?

Alan   We do have a space probe up our sleeves. It will be launched shortly by her Majesty the Queen, who, at a given signal, which is a nudge from C. P. Snow, will press a button which will then bounce a radio signal off three fixed points in the heavens – Mars, Venus, and God.

Peter   I see. So you don't feel that Britain is lagging behind other countries in this field?

Alan   Oh, no – certainly not! I mean, what other country can boast of the second largest radio telescope in the world? Pretty soon we shall have the third largest and possibly even the fourth. And all with the same equipment.

Peter   A wonderful achievement. Mr Hogg, do you feel there's life in space?

Alan   I honestly don't know. What on earth do you want to know that for! They're awful little creatures, aren't they?

Peter   No, life – *fe* – *fe*!

Alan   Oh, *life*! I'm sorry, I thought you said 'lice'. Well, I really don't know. You'll have to ask the Prime Minister about that – I really don't know.

Peter   Finally, sir, can you tell us how the atom can be harnessed for peaceful purposes?

Alan   Yes, I can do this quite easily. It has to do with the internal molecular structure of the atomic particle. Are you familiar with the atomic particle?

Peter   I'm not familiar with them, no.

Alan   I'll explain this to you. Now, within this atomic particle there are two things – the nucleus and the electron. Let me demonstrate this for you. Let's say my, ah . . . my ah . . . ah . . . my, ah . . . *left* hand, I'm sorry – my left hand is the nucleus and my right hand is the electron. Now, inside the atomic particle, the nucleus and the electron are going round each other, constantly revolving around one another – going around at a tremendous rate – you see? (*Twiddles thumbs*) There is a huge source of power here to be harnessed – and this is what we are doing in British Science today. (*Still twiddling thumbs*)

Peter Thank you very much, Mr Hogg. (*Shows Alan to rostrum. Enter Jon*) We are especially privileged this evening to have with us His Royal Highness The Duke of Edinburgh, Prince Philip. Good evening, sir. Would you like to be seated?

Jon This one here?

Peter Either one.

Jon Well I'm used to sitting on the right.

Peter Prince Philip has recently returned from Africa where he has been celebrating the independence of Kenya.

Jon Well, not exactly – *they* were.

Peter They were what?

Jon They were doing the celebrating, not me.

Peter I see.

Jon I was there in a symbolic capacity.

Peter What were you symbolising?

Jon Capitulation would be the best word for it, I suppose. Mind you, of course, I was very well received. Mr Kenyatta himself came to the airport to greet me and shook me very warmly by the throat as I got off the plane.

Peter Of course, Mr Kenyatta was at one time imprisoned by the British, wasn't he?

Jon Yes, well, that was when we thought he was a Mau Mau terrorist. Now of course we realise that he was a freedom fighter.

Peter What precisely is the difference?

Jon Very hard to tell, as a matter of fact, especially when you're being disembowelled by one. That, I gather, was how the confusion first arose.

Peter Yes, I imagine there must have been some confusion in the minds of the disembowel-ees at the time. Do you feel that Kenya is ready for independence?

Jon Oh yes, I think so. But there'll still be many links with Great Britain. For instance, Mr Kenyatta assured me that he still intends to keep my wife on the stamps.

Peter That is an encouraging sign of continuity. On the subject of your wife, sir: do you feel that the monarchy has a useful role to play in modern society?

Jon   Oh, good heavens, yes. I mean, it's the only thing that keeps me alive. God knows what I'd be doing without it. I'd probably be a ski instructor in Wengen or something ghastly like that. And besides, it does give the people something to wave at. It brings a little colour into their lives.

Peter   Of course, it costs a fair amount of money – for example, you travel everywhere by private aircraft.

Jon   Believe me, I'd love to go by public transport, but I daren't for the safety of the people.

Peter   How come?

Jon   Well, when I did once try to travel on an ordinary BOAC flight, everybody crowded up to my end of the plane to have a look at me with the result that the wretched thing became lopsided and I had to keep running back and forth to prevent us from going straight into the sea.

Peter   How public spirited of you. Finally, Prince Philip, we would all like to congratulate you on the fact that in the spring you are going to be a father again.

Jon   Thank you, yes, my wife, so to speak, is in the Royal Family way.

Peter   Yes – and we'll say goodnight with that characteristic joke.

Jon   There's nothing funny about a fourth child, I can assure you.

Peter   Not a joke. Merely a play on words – goodnight . . . there, I think we are safe now. If you would like to go up and join Mr Hogg I'm sure you two must have a great deal to talk about.

Peter goes off. Jon joins Alan on the rostrum. Slight pause

Alan   Hello, sir – have a drink.

Jon   Thank you . . . my health.

Civil War
additional material

In the Broadway version, the following material was added after Jon's speech on p. 81 'Oh dear, we'll have to take this one.'

Dudley   I would like to ask a question if I might?

Peter and Alan, simultaneously.

Peter Please do – of course we must have a question before we can give you an answer . . . The whole purpose of this meeting is to answer any questions which may help members of the audience on the subject of Civil Defence . . . but as you should know we can't give you an answer until we receive a question from you. That's the whole concept of this particular period of the meeting is to have a question followed by an answer from us . . .

Alan That's what we're here for, to answer any questions which you might have on Civil Defence . . . the government as you know wants the general public to be familiar with the problems of Civil Defence . . . The purpose is to familiarise the layman with the jungle of regulations and to deal with the complex problems of Civil Defence as we know it today . . .

Jon   I'll have to go along with that, too, I suppose.

Long pause.

Dudley No, no – do go on.
Peter As we've already explained to you, we can't go on until we get a question.
Alan An answer without a question is like a . . .
Peter A ship without a sail . . .
Dudley A rose without a thorn . . .
Alan A cat without a tail . . .
Peter A cow without an udder . . .
Dudley A cloud without a sky . . .
Alan A horse without a cart . . .
Dudley A puppy without its mummy . . .
Peter A what?
Dudley A puppy without its mummy.
Peter How disgustingly sentimental.
Dudley Well, a puppy, up to a certain age, without its mummy.
Alan At what age do puppies leave their mummies?
Peter Well, it depends on the dog. Weaning periods vary from breed to breed. For instance, I know the Dalmatian is a very long weaner.
Alan Oh, no, you're thinking of the Dachshund.
Peter No, I'm not. I never do if I can help it. I'm referring to the length of the weaning time, not the footage of the animal.

Dudley Of course, the Chihuahua is a very short weaner. Ten minutes and he's off.
Peter That's very quick.
Dudley My name for the Chihuahua is a teeny-weaner. Ha ha ha . . .
Peter Don't they call them 'Chihuahua-huas'?
Dudley No – there's only two 'huas' per doggie.
Peter I know my Aunt Beryl breeds them and she calls them 'Chihuahua-huas'.
Alan Oh, but your Aunt Beryl has a terrible stutter.
Peter Yes, I think you're probably right as she refers to her Pekinese as her 'Pekinese-nese-nese'.
Dudley Have you got a doggie?
Alan Have I got a doggie? No, I haven't got a doggie. (*To Peter*) Have you got a doggie?
Peter Ah – yes.
Dudley What kind is it?
Peter It's a Borghound – it's a foot long and three feet high.
Alan Are you sure it's a dog?
Peter Well, it shouts and yelps and it's completely covered with hair.
Dudley What do you call it?
Peter Anything that comes to mind.
Jon I wonder if I might interrupt here – am I at the right meeting?
Peter You'll have to search your own mind for that answer, Sir Basil.
Jon Well, I thought I was here to speak on Civil Defence.
Alan Well, of course that is the purpose of this meeting.
Peter Perhaps it would be better if we had a question on Civil Defence. Have you got a question on Civil Defence?
Dudley Yes, I think I can rustle one up. Rustle rustle – my little joke, ha ha.
Alan Have you a question?
Dudley Yes. Shall I fire straight ahead?
Peter Yes, by all means.
Dudley All right, here goes then.

Resume main version of sketch from – 'Dudley: Following the nuclear holocaust . . .' on p. 81.

3. A selection of additional material from the earlier versions

Edinburgh
Jim's Inn (*Cook, Miller*)

Cambridge
The Judge (*Cook*)
All Right, So It Does Not Whistle (*Miller*)
Under Canvas (*Miller, Cook*)
One Leg Too Few (*Cook*)

Jim's Inn*

Dart board, darts, table and tankards. Dudley ('Jim') leaning chummily over bar throughout. Jon ('Basil') and Peter ('Nigel') at the bar.

Jon	Hello, Nige.
Peter	Hello, Bas.
Jon	What's yours?
Peter	Pint of foamy.
Jon	Pint of foamy, Jim, and a pint of the usual for me. You know, Nige, something you haven't thought of, if you buy a pint of foamy a day, cash down, you stand to gain.
Peter	Give you a game.
Jon	Jim, you going to referee the game?
Peter	Down the hatch!
Jon	Cheers.
Peter	Excuse me mentioning it, I didn't know you could run to a tie like that, Bas. That tie must have set you back fifteen guineas. How much was it, then?
Jon	No, I'm rather pleased to see your eye lighting on my tie because, in fact, it wasn't anywhere near fifteen guineas.
Peter	How much was it?

* In the early days of commercial television there were a number of advertising magazines in which mention of commercial products was slipped into supposedly normal conversations. The practice was intended to get round the restrictions on time allowed to advertisements as such and was discontinued in 1963; *Jim's Inn* was the best-remembered of them.

Jon   Drink up and I'll tell you . . . three and six. (*Peter registers disbelief*) All right, let's ask old Jim. He's a downy one. (*To Dudley*) What would you say this tie I'm sporting cost?

Peter   Fifteen pounds?

Jon   Or three-and-six?

Dudley   Five shillings.

Jon   Well, it's on the cheap side of fifteen guineas.

Peter   Well, where did you get it?

Jon   Right-ho. I got it at Arthur Purvis, Marine Parade, Gorleston.

Peter   Sorry, Bas, I'm a bit hard of hearing – could you repeat that?

Jon   It's a Dacron tie in three part colours and it's going at three-and-six from Arthur Purvis, Marine Parade, Gorleston.

Peter   Mind if I take it off? . . . (*Does so*) Arthur Purvis, Marine Parade, Gorleston. Stone's throw from the number 15 bus.

Jon   Arthur Purvis. Come on and drink up. Good gracious me – out of the corner of my eye I thought you were wearing a good cashmere.

Peter   I'm glad you thought it was a cashmere but it's not.

Jon   I'd put my money on it being a cashmere.

Peter   You'd lose your money, Bas, it's a Nablock Histamine Non-Iron Oven-Dry Visco-Static Dynaflo, all designed to make a nice sweater with peak purchasing power.

Jon   Jim, what do you think Nige is sporting there by way of cashmere?

Dudley   Who made it, Nige, and is it costly?

Peter   Strangely enough it is made by Samuel Levi and Son who sell it at the ludicrous price of £1 4s. Samuel Levi – the Empire's largest clothier.

Jon   I suppose they must employ Japanese Sweated Labour. So it can be bought at Japanese Sweated Labour Workshops, 18 Marine Parade, Gorleston.

Peter   Another pint of foamy, Jim.

Dudley   Where can I pick that up again?

Jon   All right, the jersey Nige is wearing, which I made myself appear an awful dunderhead over in thinking a costly cashmere, is, in fact, put out by the Japanese Sweated Labour Workshops, 18 Marine Parade, Gorleston. And a snip at £1 4s.

Peter   Oh dear, one of my costly shoelaces has bust. I'll bend down and tie it. Suddenly my eyes light upon your trousers, and it seems to me that your trousers, and the jacket that goes with them, would seem to have set you back five hundred pounds.

Jon	Well, I won't say you're a complete cretin, but the suit is, in fact, priced at one hundred and eighty guineas.
Peter	180 guineas! Would you mind slipping out of it so I can take a peek?
Jon	No. (*Takes suit off*) Another pint of the old foamy.
Peter	Where did you come by this suit?
Jon	Old Nige's face is going to be red when ole' Nige sees that my suit was picked up at our friend Arthur Purvis of Gorleston.
Peter	I couldn't help overhearing you. Purvis again. What value that man packs into his shop.
Jon	He certainly does. Look at these shoes, with the wedge toe. (*Takes shoes off*)
Peter	It's a lovely design, Bas.
Jon	I thought the lines would catch your eye.
Peter	They can't have cost a penny under £167,000.
Jon	Well, as a matter of fact, Nige, they did. They cost exactly a penny under that sum. The reason why he's able to run a line like this is, of course, that Purvis and Purvis alone has the courage to use violence on his workers.
Peter	Yes, he cudgels them into greater efforts every year. And I believe his electricity is provided by old women rushing after bread in treadmills. Hello hello hello . . . my eyes are suddenly drawn – pint of foamy, Jim – to your Hoxitron Flexines. (*Indicates Jon's underpants*)
Jon	I'm glad your eyes are drawn to them, Nige, they are a costly-looking piece of raiment. And any man would be proud to gird his loins with these loin-clinging loin-cloths.
Peter	How much did these cost you? £59 million?
Jon	They *were* £59 million, but they managed to cut them to fourpence-halfpenny and I pounced on them at Arthur Purvis's store at the Marine Parade, Gorleston.
Peter	Well, do you mind slipping them off?
Dudley	Time, gentlemen, please.

The Judge

Peter Cook solo

. . . It could have been me. But I couldn't have been a Judge.
I could have been a Judge if I'd had the Latin. It's one thing
I never had. I was all torn away from school at an early age. I

was all torn away, torn away I was, by force of circumstances. I was torn away at nine and I was down the mine at nine at seven. I was down the mine at nine, at seven in the morning, working from seven to nine down the mine. At nine at seven to nine, from nine to seven and I was all at sixes and sevens down the mine at nine. That is where I was, down the mine, all down there in the dark I was . . . and what I know is all self-taught. Brought on myself through channels of knowledge what I have got in my brain. By myself all self-taught I was. What I have garnered by my own – like Geography. I like Geography. I like it because I like what it teaches, it teaches Venezuela. It's my favourite country. Venezuela is all red. It's all red in Venezuela because I know . . . I'm not saying that in Venezuela the whole aspect of the landscape is totally red. I'm not saying that every particle of dust out in Venezuela is really red in hue. I expect it's just an approximate optical representation, but it's the sort of thing that goes on down there. Shouldn't think it's entirely accurate, not down to one millionth of an inch. What I taught myself is self-taught. About Perseus and the Myth, what was trailing along behind him. He trailed along as a safeguard and a string of Gethsemane. You did the long string of Gethsemane? He trailed along as a safe-guard and came across this labyrinth. And there was waiting this one-eyed monster what hit you with it. The one-eyed minute minnow all scaly and horrible only an inch long; it was so small you never came across it. All ready to leap up your nostril. But Perseus was not abashed. He went straight in with his scimitar what he got from Jason. He went in and smit it and that minnow was disconcerted. It was minute and Perseus got it whack on the top of the head and it died. And that is how the myth sprung up . . . about Perseus and his wife in the Garden of Gethsemene, and that is why I couldn't be a Judge. That is how it happened. But it's not enough to be a Judge. All bits of knowledge brought on me by myself. You got to have Latin. I have tried to be a Judge. I went up to the Assizes place where the sentences keep going on. I went in and said, 'Excuse me, I want to be a Judge.' They said, 'Clear off, you haven't got the Latin!' But I came back five minutes later on a different tack. I said, 'I am a Judge. I've mislaid my robes, let me in.' And they said, 'Clear off, you're the same

stupid nit what was here five minutes ago.' So I never got to
be a Judge. I never got to the Assizes. I never got to have the
sentences and I never got the Latin . . . whoo . . . You notice
I suddenly went 'whoo' for no apparent reason 'whoo'?
Suddenly right out of the blue. I like to go 'whoo' every whoo
now and whoo then. That's what I got from being down the
mine at nine. I was down there all in the dark and suddenly I
was wandering about and lying there I saw the corpse. It was
terrible and horrible all dark there and frightening. And ever
since then I've been going 'whoo' unexpectedly and there is
another reason why I couldn't be a Judge. I don't think a
physical defect which causes you to go 'whoo' is particularly
funny. If *you* had cause to go 'whoo' you wouldn't greatly care
for it, I can tell you. 'Titter, titter' there every time I go
'whoo'. And I couldn't be a Judge. Destroying the Dignity of
the Court. I might be up there, all legally personified in the
robes on me. I might be up there saying 'I sentence you to
"whoo"!' and patting them on the head like I'd like to. And
you see the trouble is that under British law it would have to
stand. It would have to stick by it and all over the country in
those dark cells they would be going 'whoo'. So I couldn't be
a Judge. I never got able to be in the Assizes. I'd like to have
been a Judge. I don't grudge you what you have had. I don't
grudge you your advantage . . . hello . . . I wonder where he
went.

All Right, So It Does Not Whistle

Jonathan Miller solo

Primrose Hill. One of the many regulations controlling
behaviour on Primrose Hill, the following should cramp the
style of the most eccentric only. It is forbidden to wash
clothes, let off fireworks, perform military revolutions, and lie
in obscene postures. All this seems Perfectly Clear.
Regulation 13 is not quite so clear. No one, it says, is to
lunge on Primrose Hill without permission. Lunging, it
appears, is in fact letting a horse run round you on a leading
rein. I did not know this at the time I conceived this idea.
    The scene is Primrose Hill early in the morning. Among
the spiny machinery of the hawthorn trees. There is no-one

else about apart from the gulls with their slick cosmetic faces. Suddenly a pin-striped figure enters. Surreptitiously, he lunges. (*Lunges*)

Suddenly, before you can say Jack Rubinstein, out from behind a hawthorn tree steps a brown municipal figure of a park keeper wagging a brown municipal finger.

'Sorry, Sir, no can do, you lunged just then, didn't you? No can do, sir. However, this is essentially a permissive society so the council has included a liberal provision in the regulations saying, "No one may lunge on Primrose Hill *without permission*". That leaves it open to you to pay a visit to the Borough Surveyor's office to get yourself a lunging licence.'

The scene is the Borough Surveyor's office, where the Borough Surveyor . . . surveys the borough.

'Oh Gawd, what a boring borough.' (*Knock*)

'Hello hello, I can see what you want even before you open your mouth. You wanting a lunging licence, I say to myself. Am I right, sir? Now how many times a day do you want to lunge?'

'Well, I hadn't thought of it numerically, exactly. But I suppose seventeen times would embrace even my most exuberant appetite in that direction.'

'Good. I write out a lunging licence. "I may lunge seventeen times a day if I want to." That leaves it open to you not to want to. The mind is very open. Happy lunging, sir.'

There is absolutely no way of finishing this so I'll have to go off.

Under Canvas

Jon   Ladies and Gentlemen, the Palazzo Breschiatelli welcomes to its spacious colonnades all those exhausted with the *ennui* induced by the *hoi polloi* in the galleries of the somewhat *passé* Vichy Palace. Here may the discerning traveller, as did Ruskin, gain spiritual *nourriture* from the sweet painterly disarray of these galleries. We enter the Palazzo *palpitante* with anticipation. Here Proleski's baroque Introitus, whose fluted Corinthian in gilt and gesso startles the *blasé* twentieth-century eye with its *gaieté et distance*. We turn into Bunty's grand gallery and are affronted *subito*, as it were, by Alfresco Gatz's enormous arrogant canvas 'The Explosion of the Queen of Sheba'. Its *grandoeuvre* moves us with its instant *chiaroscuro* and by the erotic ambience which flows like some enormous succubus above the pungent figures of the Queen and her retinue. The luminous haunches of the petulant nymphs in the verdant foreground lead one's eye *molto vivace* into the caerulean *quattrocento* perspective where *putti volati* surmount the scene with naughty *insouciance* . . . whoops!

Enter Peter.

Jon	I say, I say, who's that by?
Peter	It's an early Constable nude.
Jon	Oh! I didn't know that Constable did nudes.
Peter	Oh, he did, he did indeed. Constable did nudes incessantly.
Jon	I always thought that Constable was a landscape painter.
Peter	Good God no, you mustn't run away with the idea that Constable was a landscape painter . . . The thing that Constable really enjoyed doing was painting in the nude. The nude was Constable's life. Take 'The Hay Wain', for example.
Jon	'The Hay Wain' is surely a landscape.
Peter	You cannot be more wrong. 'The Hay Wain' was originally entitled 'Passionate Breasts'. To satisfy the stringent moral code of his day Constable was forced, much against his will, to fill in his breasts with a load of old hay. Behind the hay naked women are struggling to get out. It's the same with all his paintings. The painting has recently been cleaned at the National Gallery, and the hay's away and the breasts stand out a mile.
Jon	That's very interesting – and who is the young lady?
Peter	The young lady who modelled for Constable was Alice Lauderdale, who was the young lady who came in and 'did' for Constable – practically any woman would do for Constable. She, in any case, used to come in and dust around in the nude, and Constable would get her down on the canvas and immortalise her. As you see, in most of his paintings of Alice he has been forced to disguise her as arable land.
Jon	Well, you can illustrate it with the next painting, 'Waverloe Park', which I have always thought, in my naïve way, to be a lovely landscape.
Peter	Goodness me, no, 'Waverloe Park' is a most violently erotic composition. It is, in fact, a scene of over five thousand

extremely detailed young women indulging in what cannot even be described. Look here, for example, behind this laurel bush is a very sturdy wench displaying her very obvious charms to all who pass her by. Just look at those fantastic pendulous breasts – Constable's breasts are astonishing – I think most critics are agreed that Constable's handling of breasts is out of this world, but some maintain he falls down on his thighs. I personally have an enormous admiration for Constable's *corpus dementi*. It is very sad I think that some of Constable's best breasts have been obfuscated in this prudish way. No other Victorian painter could touch Constable on his breasts. Lord Cheviot, a great wit of the time, once commented, standing in front of this very picture, 'Cleanliness is next to Godliness, but nudity is next to Constable.'

Jon   This opens up new vistas about Victorian times in general.

Peter   Let us move on into the Turners.

Jon   I think I'll stay here with the Constables, soaking up the atmosphere.

He is left on stage, scrubbing.

One Leg Too Few

Peter   Miss Rigby! Stella, my love! Would you send in the next auditioner, please, Mr Spiggott I believe it is.

Enter Dudley, hopping energetically on one leg.

Peter   Mr Spiggott, I believe?

Dudley   Yes – Spiggott by name, Spiggott by nature. (*Keeps hopping*)

Peter   Yes . . . if you'd like to remain motionless for a moment, Mr Spiggott. Please be stood. Now, Mr Spiggott, you are, I believe, auditioning for the part of Tarzan.

Dudley   Right.

Peter   Now, Mr Spiggott, I couldn't help noticing almost at once that you are a one-legged person.

Dudley   You noticed that?

Peter   I noticed that, Mr Spiggott. When you have been in the business as long as I have you come to notice these little things almost instinctively. Now, Mr Spiggott, you, a one-legged man, are applying for the role of Tarzan – a role which traditionally involves the use of a two-legged actor.

Dudley Correct.
Peter And yet you, a unidexter, are applying for the role.
Dudley Right.
Peter A role for which two legs would seem to be the minimum requirement.
Dudley Very true.
Peter Well, Mr Spiggott, need I point out to you where your deficiency lies as regards landing the role?
Dudley Yes, I think you ought to.
Peter Need I say with over much emphasis that it is in the leg division that you are deficient.
Dudley The leg division?
Peter Yes, the leg division, Mr Spiggott. You are deficient in it – to the tune of one. Your right leg I like. I like your right leg. A lovely leg for the role. That's what I said when I saw you come in. I said, 'A lovely leg for the role.' I've got nothing against your right leg. The trouble is – neither have you. You fall down on your left.
Dudley You mean it's inadequate?
Peter Yes, it's inadequate, Mr Spiggott. And, to my mind, the British public is just not ready for the sight of a one-legged ape-man swinging through the jungly tendrils.
Dudley I see.
Peter However, don't despair. After all, you score over a man with no legs at all. Should a legless man come in here demanding the role, I should have no hesitation in saying, 'Get out, run away.'
Dudley So there's still a chance?
Peter There is still a very good chance. If we get no two-legged actors in here within the next two months, there is still a very good chance that you'll land this vital role. Failing two-legged actors, you, a unidexter, are just the sort of person we shall be attempting to contact telephonically.
Dudley Well . . . thank you very much.
Peter So my advice is, to hop on a bus, go home, and sit by your telephone in the hope that we will be getting in touch with you. (*Showing Dudley out*) I'm really sorry I can't be more definite, but as you realise, it's really a two-legged man we're after. Good morning, Mr Spiggott.

Dudley goes off.

[***Peter** Now, Miss Rigby, perhaps you'd show Mr Stanger in. (*Enter Alan or Jon*) Ah, good morning Mr Stanger. Now I believe you are applying for the role of Long John Silver.]

*Section in square brackets cut when the sketch was performed in the 1964 Broadway version.

4. The gramophone records

BEYOND THE FRINGE – extracts, recorded at the Fortune Theatre, London, July 1961. Bennett, Cook, Miller, Moore.
12″ mono LP Parlophone PMC 1145
Re-issued: mono LP EMI One-up OUM 2151, published 1976.

Royal Box; The Heat-Death of the Universe; Bollard;
Deutscher Chansons; T.V.P.M.; Aftermyth of War; Real Class;
Little Miss Britten; Black Equals White; Take A Pew; The End of the World.
(Some of these sketches – in particular 'Aftermyth of War' – have been cut.)

'Take A Pew' was included in the compilation LP 'COMEDY FROM "FUN AT ONE"'.
12″ stereo LP BBC records REB 371, musicassette RMC 371, published 1979.

BEYOND THE FRINGE – ORIGINAL BROADWAY CAST: recorded in America, 1962 cast as above.
USA and UK 12″ mono LP Capitol W1792, published 1963.
USA 12″ stereo LP Capital SW 1792, imported into UK on Capitol ST11654.

Bollard; The Sadder and Wiser Beaver; Deutscher Chansons;
Take a Pew; Aftermyth of War; Sitting on the Bench;
And the Same To You (Moore piano solo); Portrait From Memory;
So That's The Way You Like It; The End of the World.

'The End of the World' and 'Sitting on the Bench' released on mono 7″ single, Parlophone 45-R 4969, published 1963.

'Sitting on the Bench' and 'And The Same To You' released on mono E.P. Parlophone GEP 8940, together with 'Duddly Dell' and 'Strictly For The Birds' by the Dudley Moore Trio; published 1965.

BEYOND THE FRINGE '64 – ORIGINAL BROADWAY CAST. Recorded in America; Bennett, Cook, Moore, Whitehead.
USA 12″ LP Capitol W2072 (mono), SW2072 (stereo), published 1964.
Not released in UK.

Home Thoughts From Abroad; The English Way of Death;
The Weill Song; Royal Box; One Leg Too Few;
Two English Songs (Little Miss Britten/Old Meg She Was A Gypsy);
Lord Cobbold/The Duke (Studio Five Interviews); Real Class;
A Piece of My Mind (The Heat-Death of the Universe); The Great Train Robbery.

5. Additional Music for the original show

Music for 'So That's the Way You Like It'

Music for 'Man Bites God'

law starts get – ting   stro_____ – ppy__,don't think   you   are

so _____ – ppy__ if you turn   the o – ther

cheek_____ .   Keep it tur –ning, tur–ning,tur–ning,tur–ning,

f

D.C. till
cut off by Jonathan

Postscripts

1. After *Beyond the Fringe* had opened at the Edinburgh Festival in August 1960 several impresarios were interested in presenting it in the West End. We rehearsed the London version at the Prince of Wales Theatre in Coventry Street, not in the auditorium but the stalls bar, which amply accommodated the podium that was the only set. It was there in April 1961 that we did a run through of the show for the benefit of Donald Albery, the leading London manager of the time. He was far from certain that the show would be a success but of one thing he was convinced: 'The fair-haired one' as he put it 'will have to go.' Reading through my contribution twenty-five years later I can see his point.

The sermon apart, what did I think I was doing? My first solo for instance, printed here in one of its several variations: can any of these earnest lecturettes have made anyone *laugh*? Mercifully I don't remember but reading them now I am torn between embarrassment at their content and admiration for the gall with which I dared to go on night after night and do them. We always referred to this first solo as my Boring Old Man sketch so I must have had some idea. I've a dreadful feeling I may have thought I was doing some good. Ah well.

On the other hand I did have a hand in some of the best stuff in the Aftermyth of War and the Civil Defence sketches, both of which helped to give the revue its topical, not to say (no, not to say . . . or at any rate without inverted commas) 'satirical' flavour. I didn't get much credit for this at the time and that rankled. Peter was so fertile and Jonathan so articulate that it was generally assumed they were responsible for the bulk of the writing. In fact Peter's was by far the largest contribution and reading it to-day, much the funniest. But he'd already had material on in the West End with *Pieces of Eight* so it wasn't his particular style of humour that made *Beyond the Fringe* so special but something about the combination of the four of us. At the time Dudley too felt his contribution was undervalued. Since those days the proper ascription of credit has always seemed to me important. Want of it is part of the raw deal of wives, male as well as female. I have just finished a script about the life of Joe Orton, murdered by his lover and teacher Kenneth Halliwell. Whereas in private Orton readily acknowledged his debt to his friend he never did so in public. No wonder Halliwell battered his brains out; there were times in those years 1961–64 when I felt like that myself.

Money is always interesting. For the original show in Edinburgh we were paid £100 each to include both writing and performance. Though in a theatre the size of the Royal Lyceum it would have been substantial, there was no author's percentage royalty. The show had hardly been costly to mount: set (none), scenery (none), props (3 chairs) . . . the entire budget was only £100. I've a feeling we even bought our own costumes.

Despite the success of that week in Edinburgh with not a seat to be had and long queues for returns, nothing seems to have alerted us to the fact that play our cards right and there was a fortune to be made here. In the worldly wisdom department we tended to look to Peter. He had already had material in West End revues and besides he wore pointed shoes and had a tailor in Old Compton Street. It followed that he must know what he was doing. In addition to the pointed shoes and the tailor in Old Compton Street Peter also had an agent. It seemed sensible, it seemed *neater* if we enrolled with him also. The agent's motto where we were concerned was 'You don't want a dollar sign over your heads'. Were Mother Teresa the client this sentiment would not have been inappropriate but with us it seemed to miss the point. It did have a point, of course though it was obscured from us at the time, in that the agent was acting not only for us but for the management as well. I remember coming away with Jonathan from the session when the contract was discussed. He had hailed a taxi; it was the first London taxi I had ever been in and riding up Half Moon Street we discussed the terms. 'They're very good' said Jonathan. 'It's ten times what I'd be receiving as a junior doctor.' It was fifteen times what I'd be receiving as a mediaeval historian but something told me even then that this was not really the point. So I kept my mouth shut, taking comfort in the illusion that the others must know what they were doing. So it is in every situation in life: somebody must know, the doctor, the surgeon, the accountant or the Prime Minister; illness, death, bankruptcy or annihilation, somebody must know. They don't, of course. They think you do.

In 1964 after the Broadway run was over we made a feeble attempt to get back some of the money we'd lost in the days of our innocence. It is a stage pop stars go through and snooker players when they sue their agents and managers in suits involving millions. Ours didn't, of course, and we never dreamed of suing. All we did was send the management a mildly rude letter. I can't remember which one of us wrote it or even if we all signed it. The time for concerted action was long since past, and anyway we were about to go our separate ways. It didn't really matter any more.

The person who suffered most from our financial naïvety was the man who had conceived the idea of *Beyond the Fringe* in the first place. In 1960 John Bassett was assistant to the director of the Edinburgh Festival, Robert Ponsonby. Bassett knew us all individually, had seen us perform and got the idea of bringing us together. I fear we were not particularly grateful for this and the management certainly weren't. Bassett received almost no recompense. Whereas we had some reason to feel aggrieved he had a great deal.

I look back on those years without nostalgia, remembering chiefly the frustrations and the embarrassments. Before the show opened in London we were interviewed on BBC TV's *To-night*. We rehearsed and recorded an extract from 'Aftermyth of War' and I stumped around stiff-legged doing a take-off of Douglas Bader. This produced a muted response in the studio and it was only when our interviewer strode in that I understood why. It was Kenneth Allsop, himself ex-RAF and with one leg into the bargain. The producer of that extract was Ned Sherrin, then one of Grace Wyndham-Goldie's up and coming young men. We sat there, the Four Horsemen of the Satirical Apocalypse while he hurriedly took us through the points he thought should be made. The countdown had already started and he was running up to the box when he looked back and said plaintively 'But what is Alan going to say?' Very little, as it turned out, and it was often like that.

This bothered me at the time but once free of *Beyond the Fringe* it bothered me not at all, seemed like a useful apprenticeship. To think, as I do now, that the less said about what one does the better is perhaps a rationalisation of not having much to say in the first place. But there was too much talk about *Beyond the Fringe* and 'satire' in general and it left me with a permanent distaste for having to explain myself or hear myself explained.

As I drew to the end of my three-year stint in the show I had no idea what I should do afterwards. Peter and Dudley had already begun to work together in the partnership that was to lead to their TV series *Not Only . . . But Also*. Jonathan was going to edit *Monitor*. Except that I had enough money to get by for a year or two the future seemed bleak. But without knowing it I'd already started heading in a different direction. For the last edition of the revue in New York I'd put together a monologue about death. It's a pretty dreadful piece and death not being the subject of lively interest it has since become the Broadway audience received it in stunned silence. My doing it in a broad Yorkshire accent can't have helped either. Still I can see in it now the germ of the television plays I went on to write ten years later. The margins of humour were beginning to interest me too. I wanted to try my hand at material that was sad as well as funny. There was no place for this in *BTF* but in my first stage play *Forty Years On*, which was part play, part revue, I did try and combine comedy and nostalgia and found the result more satisfying than anything I'd done in *Beyond the Fringe*. If *Beyond the Fringe* was the start of something it nowadays seems like another life and the person I was in it another person. It's with mixed feelings I see it resurrected.

Alan Bennett 1986

2. My memories of the first glimmerings of *Beyond the Fringe* are somewhat hazy. The first meeting we had seems to have achieved some notoriety in all of our minds, although I for the life of me cannot really remember too much about it . . . except that we were in a restaurant with John Bassett who initiated the whole idea with Robert Ponsonby. I remember feeling very small figuratively and physically at these first meetings. Jonathan was and is a powerhouse of enthusiasm and curiosity, coupled with a singeing slash of melancholia, which graces his face from time to time.

Peter Cook seemed to me a very urbane, relaxed, sophisticated young chap. Of course in many ways that assessment proved right, since Peter later established with great ease and aplomb 'The Establishment Club'. In many ways I found Peter the most approachable and relaxed – of the four of us . . . including me of course.

I don't recall much of the writing process . . . perhaps because I felt fairly futile in its creativity. However, I stayed in there, the actor-musician supplying a sense of diminution to the three other lads whose six-foot-twoness needed to have some sort of response, which I supplied with my almost eccentric five foot two.

The preparation for the show seems so murky now. The lighting man, I seem to remember, supplied us with a very practical and economical set. He lit it very well, not having to deal with too many sharp colours, since we were all dressed in grey worsted suits, white shirts and black ties. There was also an occasional dark grey sweater. We supplied props in a minimal way, which I think proved to be a very useful element in the show's success. For a long time revues had been very camp and overly colourful; our muted business suits maybe afforded a welcome contrast to the revue fare of Shaftesbury Avenue.

The work was done, much to my fairly disguised humiliation, since I was not able to participate in any way that could be hailed as helpful. I had to win my laurels eventually it seemed through my abilities as a performer – especially as a reactor, since most people who invented a line kept it! Therefore, I was a mildly mute person on stage while the others flourished their wares shamelessly! I think that my musical efforts were viewed somewhat patronisingly – certainly with little comprehension – dare I say it . . . I was a rehearsal pianist.

I remember vaguely the night before the first performance at Edinburgh and the actual night itself. I had to construct a solo – we all had one solo during this shortened version of *Beyond the Fringe* – and I still hadn't got one that I felt was satisfactory. I decided to write a sonata movement using one of the silliest songs that I knew and one of the greatest composers. It seemed to be a marriage which would give some spicy instances of satire. Thus, I chose the 'Colonel Bogey March' as used in the film *Bridge Over the River Kwai* and worked it in the style of Beethoven. I did it very loosely in first movement form (sonata form) and I remembered some time later in London, when my professor (Jack Westrup from Oxford) came to see the show and commented he was longing for a 'development section'! I had to point out that in the interests of comedic economy, no such luxury could be afforded. I composed this piece quickly and directly the night before the show and remember being somewhat delighted at the response of the audience . . . especially at an extended ending that aped the Beethoven ending of the Fifth Symphony. I improvised endless codas, to the delight of the audience it seemed, until one day the construction of the thing became thoroughly solid. Since then I have played that item to death many times!

They were exotic years and exotic experiences . . . I don't think I ever had such grand excitement. It was everything I had ever wanted . . . to be on stage in a revue. The response and environments could not have been better and I came back finally from America feeling that I had probably achieved everything I ever wanted to – until I found that the prospect of appearing on TV was possible. Peter and I in fact had been able to get a very good relationship going in the last year of *Beyond the Fringe* on Broadway. We had such a grand time that obviously the temptation grew to repeat the experience on television, which we eventually did in our programmes *Not Only . . . But Also*.

Alan Bennett and I had been very friendly at the beginning of the American run, having dinner every night at a place called Barbetta's, which was just west of Eighth Avenue on 45th or 46th Street. Alan and I used to go to this restaurant, always greeted by the doorman who had a very thick foreign accent – I don't quite know where he came from – and he greeted us with the immortal lines: 'Ah, Mr Moore, Mr Cook . . . Behind the Fridge.' Eventually Peter Cook and I usurped this garbled title and used it for a subsequent two-man show which we did in Australia, New Zealand and England. When we finally came to Broadway we changed the title to *Good Evening* and I'm happy to report we had a great success doing that show there too.

Dudley Moore 1986

3. I never had it so good. As far as I was concerned, the wonderful old showbiz fraud had got it right. I had a flat in Battersea, a Hillman Convertible and the chance to show off every night.

'Don't jeopardise your career by working with these three amateurs' had been the advice of my agent who shall remain nameless (but Donald Langdon is pretty close).

It was a peculiar business assembling the show. Only Dudley and I seemed to want to do it; the other two were perpetually struggling with their consciences. Should Jonathan desert medicine for this frivolous pursuit? Would Alan forsake Oxford and Medieval History for the transient glamour of the Fortune Theatre? Would they ever make up their minds?

In the early days Alan was delightfully shockable. It gave me enormous pleasure to come up with some piece of smut and watch him writhe and moan in agony or amusement, stuffing his handkerchief into his mouth. This handkerchief technique must have had its uses. Sometimes it was employed to stifle his own laughter, at others to conceal his vexation. It was quite hard to tell whether he was having a fit of the giggles or in an almost terminal state of irritation. Happily, he eventually became as filthy minded as the rest of us.

I look back on the show with nothing but pleasure. I can remember very few rows, though there was one occasion when Jonathan hurled a teatray across the dressing room in a fit of pique with, I think, Alan. Possibly the latter had been chewing his handkerchief in a insolent manner.

At another time Jonathan became enraged at me. It was often my wont to interrupt the Philosophy Sketch by staggering on as an ancient retainer to deliver some incongruous piece of news. One night Rachel Miller was backstage with their newborn son. Grabbing the baby from the willing Mrs Miller I wandered on saying: 'Excuse me Sir, your wife's just given birth to this' to which I think Jonathan replied: 'Go away and put it in the fridge'. I thought this a highly successful piece of improvisation but at the interval Jonathan reprimanded me severely. 'You might have dropped it!' he said. Never having wittingly dropped a baby in my life I felt a little aggrieved. (He was the one who was clumsy with props.) I seem to remember at a later date carrying Dudley on and saying: 'I've discovered this man in bed with your wife and so I shot him' to which Jonathan rather cruelly replied: 'Oh well, just drop him anywhere.'

As the show went on I began to enjoy the 'digressions' more than the written text. I particularly looked forward to Dudley interrupting the Civil Defence Sketch. The barmy ad-libbed questions and answers, usually nothing to do with the subject, were the highlight of the evening for me. I think it was this kind of daft random backchat that led to the two of us working together on television.

There is only one depressing side effect of re-reading the text – I may have done some other things as good but I am sure none better. I haven't matured, progressed, grown, become deeper, wiser, or funnier. But then, I never thought I would.

Peter Cook 1987

Methuen Humour Classics

Charles Addams	ADDAMS AND EVIL
Alphonse Allais	A WOLF IN FROG'S CLOTHING
	Selected, translated and introduced by Miles Kington
Noël Coward	THE LYRICS OF NOËL COWARD
	A WITHERED NOSEGAY
A. P. Herbert	UNCOMMON LAW
	MORE UNCOMMON LAW
Paul Jennings	GOLDEN ODDLIES
Jerome K. Jerome	THREE MEN IN AN OMNIBUS
	Illustrated by Posy Simmonds
Osbert Lancaster	THE LITTLEHAMPTON SAGA
Edward Lear	THE NONSENSE VERSE OF EDWARD LEAR
	Illustrated by John Vernon Lord
Tom Lehrer	TOO MANY SONGS BY TOM LEHRER
	Illustrated by Ronald Searle
Frank Muir and Denis Norden	THE COMPLETE AND UTTER 'MY WORD!' COLLECTION
Ogden Nash	CANDY IS DANDY: THE BEST OF OGDEN NASH
S. J. Perelman	THE LAST LAUGH
	THE MOST OF S. J. PERELMAN
R. E. Raspe	THE ADVENTURES OF BARON MUNCHAUSEN
	Illustrated by Ronald Searle
W. C. Sellar and R. J. Yeatman	1066 AND ALL THAT
	AND NOW ALL THIS
James Thurber	LET YOUR MIND ALONE!
	THE MIDDLE-AGED MAN ON THE FLYING TRAPEZE
	MY WORLD – AND WELCOME TO IT